To Dave & Gloria

Precious frien[d]
always gave me gu[...]
advice, ranging from writing
to life itself. A couple
who typify what love is all
about: caring and sharing
through good times as
well a times that
were difficult. I
admire you both

[signature]

OPEN WIDE AND LAUGH

FUN AT THE DENTIST? WHY NOT?

DR. BERNARD G. PARK

authorHOUSE®

AuthorHouse™
1663 Liberty Drive
Bloomington, IN 47403
www.authorhouse.com
Phone: 1 (800) 839-8640

Published by AuthorHouse 06/30/2017

ISBN: 978-1-5246-9874-4 (sc)
ISBN: 978-1-5246-9872-0 (hc)
ISBN: 978-1-5246-9873-7 (e)

Print information available on the last page.

Any people depicted in stock imagery provided by Thinkstock are models,
and such images are being used for illustrative purposes only.
Certain stock imagery © Thinkstock.

This book is printed on acid-free paper.

Because of the dynamic nature of the Internet, any web addresses or
links contained in this book may have changed since publication and
may no longer be valid. The views expressed in this work are solely those
of the author and do not necessarily reflect the views of the publisher,
and the publisher hereby disclaims any responsibility for them.

INTRODUCTION

Open wide and laugh were four words that could not have been put together to form a meaningful clinical sentence when this narrative began in September 1957. It would have had an oxymoronic sound to it. Dentistry was a vaunted profession, the mention of which conjured up an image of a stern-looking man wearing a white starched snap-buttoned dental gown standing next to an uncomfortable-looking drab black dental chair, and with a belt and pulley system driven dental engine looming on the other side like a Martian mini-monster. Added to the picture was the stark white hygienic-looking form of a cabinet containing sterilized instruments in the background, its counter top laden with aluminum containers filled with gauze pads, vials containing dental anesthetic, scissors and long-handled clamps. And there was always that powerful smell, the ever-present odor of oil of cloves. And if there was a dental hygienist in the office she also wore a starched white uniform, white shoes and a cap on her head. Even the cap was rigid. A formal and foreboding environment. A den of discomfort. Ironic, for while representing an enterprise that promoted healthy smiles, very few were ever seen in that setting.

It was a relatively quiet time in America. Post-war prosperity had taken hold. President Eisenhower has often been described as a care-taker president, and his critics would usually offer one complaint, his frequent golf games. He introduced the interstate highway system as a defense measure, and at the same time made travel in the country easier than ever. The suburbs were growing, and the dream of a house, children, and a car in the driveway was within reach of most young folks. Many schools in our southern states were still segregated, and change would not come until the momentous Brown vs. Board of Education case was heard a few years later. The great debates in this country were whether butter or margarine was better, and when would television be seen in color and would it be easily affordable. The Brooklyn Dodgers and New York Giants both moved to California, police radar made its appearance on our roads, and the first nuclear plant for production of electricity opened in Pennsylvania. Rumblings in the Middle East, although inherently dangerous, were short-lived and resolved without fear of becoming a major conflagration.

Half of Americans had never heard of Vietnam, and many of the other half would have had difficulty locating that country on a map. Russia embarked on a program that they hoped would lead to travel through space. Our national pride was mustered, and an awakened drive for scientific progress began. Children were taught, and then demonstrated, respect for authority for both parents and teachers. Television audiences were always seen to be composed of men dressed in jackets and ladies adorned in current style. A medical visit conjured up an image of a physician in his white jacket, seated and writing down his examination findings in cursive script, using a fountain pen on a pad of white paper, while listening to every word spoken by the patient. Pharmacists compounded as well as dispensed medication, and were so respected that in many states they were called "doc." Education was important, and the professions were held in high esteem. The insurance companies were just beginning to exert some influence in several medical fields, and the Medicare Act was still almost a decade away. Humor was ever-present. One could access the parodies of Stan Freberg on the radio, the antics of Martin and Lewis in the movies, the slapstick of Red Skelton on television, and the cerebral comedy of Bob Newhart on records. But humor in a dental office...nonexistent.

It was a moment in the clinic at Penn Dental School when I overheard a brief conversation that taught me a valuable lesson, and perhaps was the greatest factor that eventually led to the unfolding of this story. A student in the prosthetics section had examined a man who was missing several teeth, and for whom treatment consisting of replacement with a removable partial denture was indicated, both economically and biologically. The student approached the clinical instructor before proceeding with treatment, saying,"I have a partial patient." The professor's reply was a mini-lesson in human relations: "Where's the rest of him?" It was for the "rest of him" that I eventually (after getting over the initial formal and austere phase of my practice) realized the value of humor in relating to human beings. The late Dr. Wayne Dyer taught that, "If you change the way you look at things, the things you look at change." It was my goal to have my patients approach each visit with minimal trepidation, knowing that not only would we recognize and respect the individual's dignity, but also make every attempt to lessen any anxiety by using laughter as a distraction as well as a seratonin-level increaser. We could be serious, professional, light-hearted and sometimes downright silly, all in the same hour.

As I sat down to write I was fortunate to be able to recall so many lighter moments that got us all through dental school, and how I was able to use that as a template for my professional experience. Although we worked in the mouth, we knew there was a body and a mind attached to it...the "rest of him". We shared four years preparing to make life a little better for a lot of people. Therefore, it is with love and gratitude that I dedicate this book to my classmates, University of Pennsylvania School of Dentistry, class of 1961. We all bought the same ticket at the same station at the same time for the same trip, a journey that covered sixty years, or as we like to define chunks of time, seven decades. It began in the same month that a little orb named Sputnik made its way gracefully around our planet, and continued on to witness humans living and working in outer space. The continuum saw changes from a formalistic culture to one where a casual mode is now in style. And the vaunted, formal, dental profession began to allow its practitioners to relate to patients as not just people, but more importantly, as friends. We were fun-loving so many years ago, and learned that its was okay to keep and nurture that aspect of our being and indeed to make it a background for our work. Also, each one of us was, on occasion, a dental patient. We saw the profession from both sides of the mirror. And now, as I wistfully look back, I firmly believe we all somehow managed to make the once dreaded dental appointment a bit more palatable. (Pun definitely intended).

When I opened my dental practice in Colchester Connecticut in September 1963, after a tour of active duty in the Army, I found myself in a strange situation. I had been an officer, a captain, and I had a title, doctor, but my natural psyche and spirit was that of a fun-loving, sometimes bordering on iconoclastic being, who was brought up to respect people because they were individuals. Titles only defined their place on the spectrum of expected contributions to the human condition. I was a dentist! I was supposed to wear a starched, clinical-looking white garment and speak with a hint of subdued condescension to everyone except co-medical professionals, with whom I could engage in a conversational tone that smacked of self-adulation and muffled arrogance. This was a world where artificial parameters of behavior set the stage upon which emotional comfort and physical attention would be measured out to patients. Finding humor in a dental office was like spotting a ptarmigan (a bird whose plumage turns white in the winter) in the snow: if it was there one could not discover it, let alone appreciate it.

What a time of confusion. Having had four years of daily shirt and tie requirements in dental school followed by two years of prescribed military uniform guidelines (summer, winter, fatigues and dress formal) I now laugh at myself when I realize that I was so sartorially discombobulated that I was not able to go to a local Cumberland Farms store to get milk in the evening without putting on a sport jacket. What is the proper way to dress? However, and to my credit, I was not uneasy about being seen in public without a tie. I could have been a poster boy for a "lighten up" movement. This was a speed bump just before the long hair, sideburns, bell-bottom pants, bra-less movement that soon followed. So steeped in formality was I that I enjoyed hearing, "good morning Dr. Park" every day, and that was from my wife and children.

At the time I opened my office there was only one dental joke in existence, and it remained the only joke about my profession for many years. It had a life of its own. It first appeared early in my dental school career, and lived on for more than a decade:

Patient:"I don't know whether I'd rather have a tooth filled or have a baby."

Dentist:"You'd better make up your mind lady so I will know how to adjust the chair."

I heard that joke quite a few times in my early practice years, and it quickly taught me a great lesson in human behavior. When a person tells a joke he or she waits one millisecond for a response. If the jokee laughs immediately and heartily the joker is quite pleased. If the gag brings about a lesser response the teller's ego becomes slightly bruised. Transactional analysis,a method whereby social transactions are analyzed, would reveal that the patient, in telling a joke, is trying to "level the playing field" in the interaction between the lofty professional and the uncomfortable patient. I realized that I would be giving great spiritual comfort to the uneasy person sitting in my dental chair, dressed for the occasion with a large napkin draped over the front which was held in place by two menacing looking alligator clamps, and surrounded by an array of shiny instruments which can cause discomfort (we never say pain), and who is seated below eye level of the doctor. If I would respond quickly with a hearty laugh, wide smile and a few words of praise for the patient's sense of humor. The happy response which this always produced was a signal to me that the procedure could now begin.

In the 1960's all dental offices looked the same. The dental unit, with its array of angled belts and the ominous slow speed drill, was partnered with a large, operating lamp that looked somewhat like a searchlight that threatened to discover the smallest of dental deficiencies in the most remote corner of the mouth. The dark headrest and arms of the dental chair combined to display a profile of discomfort. It could easily remind one of a scene in a gangster movie where the camera zoomed in on the prison electric chair which awaited James Cagney, as a priest and the warden flanked him on his slow walk to his final destination. And the dentist was usually wearing a starched white clinical smock that was fastened across the top with a row of military-looking snaps. Instruments were arranged in a soldierly fashion, like metal warriors lined up in a precise formation on a ceramic circular table that reminded one of a sacrificial altar. Additionally, the air was filled with the ever-present scent of oil of cloves, a key ingredient in "temporary fillings" whose medicinal fragrance served as sharp contrast to the far more pleasant aroma of beef stew or bread baking in the oven or fresh brewed coffee which the patient may have just left behind because it was approaching the time for a dental visit. Within sight was the cabinet on which sat jars filled with gauze sponges and the ubiquitous bottle of alcohol. And inside the closed drawers one could imagine an array of syringes, needles, extraction forceps, and other devices which are much better kept hidden. A small radio made an attempt to provide soothing music in the background, but the program was constantly being interrupted by commercials, weather forecasts, a traffic report or sports score, plus an awareness of the the crackling sound of static in the background that was an identifying feature of most AM stations of that day.

Conversation between patient and doctor was often laconic, brief, as one hoped the visit would be. The practitioners that I knew as a youngster, while growing up in Roxbury Massachusetts, were the products of professional schools that, be it medicine, law, or any related field, somehow imbued their graduates with a an attitude of respectful aloofness. They were by-products of a post-depression era where sharp distinctions between working and professional, haves and have-nots, were not only acted out in real life, but were portrayed almost as stereotypes in the movies of that time. The doctor spoke with authority, and the patient accepted any proclamation as words of unquestioned wisdom. Orders were followed and personal dialogue was non-existent. Mentioning the term 'dental office' invoked images ranging from discomfort to hurt to pain, and, with added apprehension mixed in, sometimes even to the agony characterized by one of the most disturbing scenes in all of movie history: the film "Marathon Man" where Laurence Olivier uses a dental drill to torture Dustin Hoffman into releasing information. Somewhere deep in my psyche I perceived a different image, one where interpersonal relationships and professional training could combine to provide a practice setting where people could be treated both medically and personally in a kindhearted and non-intimidating fashion.

Aside from excellent public school preparation for college, I was fortunate (as I look back now) to have been involved in a variety of quasi-educational situations that served as a hands-on course in public relations, and provided a laboratory for evaluating methods and techniques of social interchange. I am referring to the many summer and school year part time jobs that helped pay for the ticket for my trip. During my high school years I worked in a local pharmacy as a soda jerk, and also as a lab assistant in chemistry class. Holiday vacations in college found me acting as a parking lot attendant, letter carrier for the U.S. Postal Service, and a salesman of men's shirts in Filene's Department Store in Boston. But my main source of tuition money came from the two jobs that I held concurrently for seven summers. During the day I was employed in the State House in Boston, functioning as a junior accountant in the office of Thomas Buckley, Auditor of the Commonwealth of Massachusetts. Then, at 4:30 I would take a subway train to Revere Beach, about ten miles away, where I worked as a carnival barker until midnight. The beach job involved every Saturday and Sunday. I truly believe that in those years I was exposed to, and interacted with, every type of personality in existence, and learned first hand how to deal with every aspect, both good and not so good, of the human condition. So now I was prepared for a career in dentistry.

DENTAL SCHOOL

September 1957: orientation program at the University of Pennsylvania School of Dental Medicine. The setting was a large lecture hall filled with 120 young, eager, very impressionable neophytes, who had only a vague idea of the task ahead. The composite (a pun in today's dental nomenclature) picture was that of a somber-faced group of men (plus two women!) awaiting the first official interchange between faculty and my new classmates. We were to be indoctrinated in the meaning of the exalted word professional, along with all its incumbent obligations, such as being a continual student throughout life, always dressing properly, and exhibiting personal behavior reflective of our new status in the esteemed world of respectable professions. The dean did introduce a moment of levity, saying that dental students were "the apple of every single girl's eye in Philadelphia," because unlike the medical and veterinary students, our lives would be enhanced by a work schedule that had us home in time for dinner every day, and that we would rarely be interrupted by house calls or late-hour hospital visits. In addition, we would have the ability to provide an excellent income plus gain instant social status wherever we went.

The lecture was well received, and I recall walking out of the building toward my rooming house dorm feeling more than a little bit inflated. I was a professional student, and my life is now taking me to high place of self respect. I was a member of an elite group. I had made a giant leap from my four undergraduate years at Tufts College (now University), where, as a commuting student,

I spent three hours of every school day traveling between my home in Roxbury and the campus in Medford Massachusetts... one street car, two subway trains, and one trackless trolley...each way. Now the dean's message was eagerly received, especially the "apple" part.

That first weekend I went with a group of new friends to downtown Philadelphia to have a brew or two and just get to know each other, exchanging thoughts about the coming year as well as diminishing any anxiety about the difficult program which we all faced. As a few young woman passed by we would remember the "apple" and in a not too quiet voice bandy about a few dental terms that might serve as verbal bait to get us noticed, and perhaps even spark a bit of interest. I remember distinctly throwing out the word "prosthetics" which I saw in the first semester's schedule, realizing that it sounded impressive, even though I had no idea what a prosthesis was. That moment was an epiphany. I suddenly realized that I would be able to fit a bit of light-heartedness into the implementation of my professional career, and yet still remain a continual student. Although our attempt to impress any of the Philly lassies was unsuccessful, we had a fun evening, and were ready for our first lecture on Monday morning. We would survive.

The tone of the first few weeks of my freshman year was one of muted self-assurance. We were neophytes in a professional school, one that would enable us to achieve a highly respected as well as a comfortable financial status in life. We would be part of a medical community that, pre-governmental regulations and pre-insurance dependency, was held in very high esteem. I was so aware of my new place on the cusp (pun intended) of a wonderful life that I worked very hard and, as a result, received the best grades of my life in my first semester, studying longer and more focused than I ever thought possible. I was going to make it! Serious, serious, serious. By the middle of the second semester, with the increasing belief that a sophomore year lay clearly ahead, we all began to feel a bit more at ease. Translated: fun time could be interspersed. In a lab class where our task was to carve teeth to a perfect scale from wax blocks, I kept my finished products in an empty Bufferin jar (which was part of my supplies and equipment inventory). At the end of one lab session I showed the bottle to the instructor, and without hesitation stated that I used this storage method because, "the course gave me a headache." I was doing well at the time, which energized me. The instructor managed a slow smile and even a bit of a laugh. Success! There was hope for a smile or even a chuckle in that starched-white environment!

The laboratory technique classes were designed to acquaint us with dental materials and their eventual application in treating real people. Pre-clinical courses allowed us to become acquainted with methodology and then to begin to hone our skills In one of our first prosthetic exercises our objective was to learn to take a wax impression of an object, and then create a duplicate in dental stone. The Benjamin Franklin 50 cent piece was chosen for both its size and its crisp carving on the obverse side. Our exercise consisted if wrapping the edge of the coin in wax and then flowing the properly mixed water and powder slurry onto the coin. When the stone had set, we removed the wax border and examined the cast for consistency and clarity. I remember saying to my nearby classmates that here we were into our second week of dental school, and they were already teaching us to make money!

One popular dental material produced an ironic situation. The cost of gold was approximately 36 dollars an ounce, and we were allowed to keep any scraps of the metal that remained after we had cast our crowns and inlays. Since our dental casting gold was 18 carats, in today's market the value of those remnants has increased forty-fold. Many dental students in that era fashioned the scrap gold into charms for use as gifts for friends and family or to create a bracelet for their ladies, and almost every student carved a molar in wax and then cast a gold tooth as a reminder of their early clinical skills. We had precious little money, but plenty of gold!

During our first two years some of the courses, such as anatomy, biochemistry, physiology, and cytology were taught at the medical school, which was located just a few blocks away. Some of that school's faculty considered the dental students to be a step or two beneath their own students, and subsequently treated us with more than just a small bit of condescension. The professor who was in charge of the Human Anatomy class was unashamedly the leader of the pack. Gross anatomy is a difficult enough subject without being taught by a person who sneered at almost every question asked by an anxious student. We had a preview of the year ahead when on the first day he ambled to the blackboard and wrote the word LABORATORY, and with a smile on his face doctored (pun intended) it to read LABOR/ORATORY, saying that he wanted a lot of the first part, and none of the second. His dislike of us was so evident, that he concocted a scheme at the end of the first semester which was designed to unnerve everyone. The final exam involved identification of parts of the entire body. Throughout the course we had worked in dissection teams of four students per cadaver, in a lab with thirty tables. Before the test day each student was charged with placing a numbered paper tag on one body part. Thus, although each group of four would know what structure their tags represented, the other 116 in the lab were unknown. The exam would consist of each student moving from table to table, and writing down the names of the structures on the exam sheet. Since Penn operated on an honor system (one transgression and if caught you are gone!), the labels of the rest of the class would not be revealed. There would certainly be no discussion among ourselves before exam day. Supposedly that was a good way of administering a test. The class did the tagging, and the quiz format was both rational and valid.

The next day we gathered in the lab at our own tables. With exam sheets in hand, and were told to undrape the cadavers, to identify and write down the name of the tagged structures, and move on to the next table on signal. This would continue until the entire lab had been traversed. At least we knew what our table held, so we would begin by being a bit relaxed because we knew that we had at least four correct answers. As we lifted off the carbolic-acid soaked sheet we could hear a collective gasp in the room. The instructors had changed all the tags, and replaced them with totally different labels. Macabre humor of the finest kind!

The only moment of comic relief during the entire year in that class occurred one very warm and extremely humid spring afternoon (a Philadelphia special) when the dissection was intense and the air a bit foul, when the silence was broken by a soft, mournful voice that was heard saying, "I'm dropping this and taking a lit course." Even the physiology professor struck fear in the class by announcing that studying for his final exam is always extremely difficult. "I give the same exam every year, but the answers keep changing." Were our lecture notes and textbooks up to the minute? And that was decades before the explosion of information technology.

With this authoritarian background ever-present we soon developed a strong sense of camaraderie. We were not in competition with each other. We all had the same ticket for the same ride, and a spirit of co-operation pervaded. We were able to create light-hearted moments in both our pre-clinical and lecture courses. When a professor in the biochemistry class diagramed a complex hexagonal-shaped molecule on the blackboard and asked that it be identified, one pundit exclaimed, "tri-nitro chicken wire." That brought a welcome smile from the lecturer and a moment of relief for all of us.

One favorite prank consisted of starting a rumor about a surprise exam or an upcoming difficult lab procedure, and then watching it make the rounds over the next day or two. I must confess that my roommate and I once shared "inside information" about an extremely difficult pre-clinical exam that would consist of duplicating in wax the relationship of teeth in a specific biting movement, a most formidable undertaking. The news moved around slowly, and by the time it reached us a few days later it had been altered enough and became believable enough to generate within both of us a mild state of panic. An upperclassman who knew what was happening laughed, and said that we had learned the fine distinction between "bullshit" and "horseshit"...the former being when you tell it, and the latter happens when you tell it so much that you yourself believe it.

With so much external pressure on us we had developed a willing attitude of helpfulness. Study notes were voluntarily shared, and tips for improving our lab exercises were exchanged. Everyone was willing to function as a neophyte tutor. But as a group we did not tolerate anyone who sought to gain personal advantage by pandering to or befriending the faculty, a term known then (and probably still identifiable now) as brown-nosing. However one of my classmates was so skilled in that practice and did it so often that the majority of the class soon became angry with him. Rather than confront him and show our displeasure, we devised a scheme that we knew would cure him of his disturbing addiction for good. We took an impression of a fellow classmate's very large nose, poured a model of this sizable proboscis in dental stone, and painted it brown. We sent it to the victim, at the dental school address. Outside the office of the dean was a bulletin board, where the his secretary would, on a daily basis, post notices of interest and/or importance. Any student mail addressed in care of the school was delivered to the dean's office so that notification could be posted, and the student could then pick up his mail from the secretary. Word spread quickly that the package had arrived, and a small crowd of fellow pranksters gathered at the bulletin board, seemingly to scan the notices, but actually waiting for the trap to spring. When the brown-noser retrieved his package we watched as he opened it. The laughter that echoed down the hall was loud enough to cure him of his habit. His figurative brown nose was eclipsed by his obvious red face.

Just as light chases dark, humor helped soften our stern environment. The ultimate fear of flunking out of school presented itself on occasion, but there were many mini-fears along the way. The Guidance Committee was the greatest heart-beat accelerator. It was a cluster of faculty members who were involved in each class's curriculum, and met periodically to evaluate each student group. At their meeting they would call in any student who might be having difficulty, real or perceived, and interview (interrogate?)

them, suggesting remedial action if necessary or simply issuing a warning about the dangers and consequences of under-performing. The student would then be told that re-evaluation would occur in the future. The committee's meeting schedule was not posted, but everyone quickly knew when an inquisition was being held. The pattern was always the same. In the middle of a morning clinic session one would hear a name announced over the speaker system directing that student to report to the dean's office. Since the names were always called in alphabetical order, we knew when our danger moment for investigation had passed.

One morning, as I was heading for the lavatory, I asked a classmate to stand outside the door as I went inside and to listen to the clinic loudspeakers to hear if my name was called while I was in the bathroom. When I emerged I stood at my post by the door while he then went in to relieve himself. What a pleasant memory. We were even able to laugh at it then. At no other moment in my four years at Penn was I able to comfort myself more by recalling the words of James Boswell in his biography of Samuel Johnson, when he stated that one should "consider how unimportant all this will seem a twelve-month hence." Again, being an English major does help facilitate dental education.

With that in the background, both literally and figuratively, I must confess to an indiscretion to which I had been a party oh so long ago. However, I was the facilitator, but not the beneficiary. In our histology class, which was taught at the medical school in the second semester of our freshman year, we had weekly spot quizzes. They were short and precise. We were given a glass slide that contained an embedded specimen, and by using the microscope had to identify that slice of human tissue. The slide-de-jour was a specimen cut from a section of mammary gland. I wrote down my answer quickly, and while idly glancing around, noticed that my friend who was sitting on my right was staring off into space. He appeared to be stymied by the object under examination. The look of bewilderment on his face tempted me to help him. Whispering or jotting down the answer in a note would have gotten us both into a heap of trouble. Struck with a thought,

I quietly hummed the tune of a then-current Dean Martin hit. A smile slowly moved across his face, and he quickly wrote down the correct answer. The song was "Memories Are Made Of This."

Having been born and raised in Boston (Roxbury) I did not realize, as a youngster, that I had an accent of any kind. My name was Benahd Pahk, and I lived on a third floh. I drove a cah, and on Saturdays took a bahth. As grating and unmelodious the oft-mimicked Boston accent was to others, the Philadelphia (Baltimore-Jersey) nasal twang sounded strange to me. I was often asked to say certain words, such as hahf (half) and lasah (laser). Once when I needed change I asked if anybody had "fowah quatahs for a dollah." The joshing was good natured, and when a close friend dubbed me "Boston Bernie" the nick-name stuck, and I no longer had to perform diction exercises. Thank Gawd. But now that accent is long gone. Having lived in Pennsylvania, Louisiana and then in Connecticut for the remainder of my life, any remnant of that flavorful linguistic aberration has long been deleted from my vocal computer memory. However, hearing it spoken brings back a flood of pleasant memories. And it is not musical. I can describe the discordant sound that I now hear as being akin to the melody that would be produced by a musician trying to play Mozart on a tuba. Or, as fellow Bostonian President John Kennedy might have said, a tuber.

To say that the faculty was devoid of humor would be an understatement. The serious tone that pervaded the atmosphere was played against a most sterile environment. Students wore starched white clinical gowns, white shirts and sported muted neckties. Instructors strolled about in their shiny white jackets with their names embroidered in blue script on the pocket tops, and the awesome letters DDS after their name; the ruling gentry. Walking onto the clinic floor, a patient was immediately presented with an image that only the term "white coat syndrome" could describe, bringing about a quick elevation of blood pressure. Even the so-called "elevator music" playing in the background did little to relax a person. And the starched caps on the heads of the hygienists! Ironically, in a professional school that dealt with developing a backdrop of pleasant smiles, there were precious few in that environment. I cite one example of the cheerlessness that surrounded us. I was treating a patient who had a few gum line cavities. I was placing gold foil restorations, which was a fairly common form of treatment at the time. Feeling a presence behind me, I turned quickly and saw the stern, unsmiling face of the department head, who had been observing quietly. There was not even a nod verifying his recognition of my existence. Continuing my task, I could feel pressure building up inside, but I relaxed when I realized all was going well. After a full five minutes of watching he moved on, but had to leave a parting shot. "Well Park, I guess you're not going to screw something up today." I did not drink a toast to his good health that evening.

On a rare occasion one of us would balk at being intimidated, and would offer a retort that would be considered funny in any other setting. However, in the clinic we were often afraid to cause the slightest ripple in that stern sea of unsmiling instructors. But one day a classmate broke the tension, if only for a moment. He had just completed a periodontal exam, which consisted of examining the roots of the teeth with an explorer, the so-called dreaded 'dental pick'. He detected very little calculus (tartar), and recorded his findings on the patient's record. When the instructor took up the instrument to check both the patient's condition and the student's prowess, he discovered a bit more. He proclaimed that he had just demonstrated "how an exam should be done." He then glared at the student and asked for a response. "What did that teach you?" With a burst of renewed courage my classmate looked at him, smiled, and with a bit of enthusiasm said, "you sure do know how to use an explorer."

We all learned to function well, finding comic relief joking about various instructors during weekend parties. A few were as pleasant as decorum allowed, but some of my classmates were skilled in mimicking, and that often served to release a bit of anxiety. As the middle of my senior year approached, a sense of relief was evident. The faculty appeared to be a wee bit more relaxed in their approach to the daily tasks. It was traditional at Penn for the senior class to put on a play one month before graduation, and the only limit to the script was good taste. I joined with a dozen classmates, and we wrote a play loosely based on the popular show of the day, West Side Story. We called it "Spruce Street Story." (The school address was 40th and Spruce). It opened with a humorous monologue, which I delivered. This was a strange experience, for I was given permission to wear the hallowed Instructor's Jacket. That was followed by a number of skits that allowed us to finally present to the world a compilation of our impressions of the foibles and caricatures that we had witnessed for three and one half years. The show was a cathartic event for students and faculty alike. I believe the purpose of allowing the senior class to parody the school and the faculty was to transition us back to a world where laughter was part of the daily norm. Co-incidentally (pun intended) the department heads had scheduled a meeting a few days later with my class to say a pre-graduation goodbye. Finally, a ray of sunshine entered that lecture room. The head of the main clinic wished us success, and as a small, almost practiced smile worked its way across his lips, he uttered the only amusing line that we had heard from any member of that esteemed group in four years: "Well, I guess we made a helluva big deal out of thirty-two teeth!" And then his smile widened, as though he surprised himself with his ability to act in a lighthearted fashion toward a group that he had figuratively terrorized and who were now about to become his colleagues.

So that chapter of my life ended. To convey the relief and joy which I felt at graduation, I have often told the story of my response when people would ask me to cite the happiest day of my life (excluding the births of three children, six grandchildren, plus one divorce). I would always tell them that it was the day when a young man named Carroll Andres graduated from Penn Dental. That quick answer always produced blank stares. So I would explain it in a very simple fashion. It was commencement day, and we were lined up alphabetically for the final ceremony, the presentation of our diplomas. There I was, standing with my classmates, quite anxiously awaiting that long-cherished moment. As the roll call began, the dean announced the first name: "Doctor Carroll Andres." I breathed a sigh of relief. I knew that I had made it. They called the first guy in line "doctor." And I was standing in that same line!

As a final note to highlight the unpleasantness generated by many of the teaching staff during those four intense years, we broke with a long-standing tradition. It had been customary for each graduating class to dedicate their yearbook to a faculty member who had been deserving of recognition, by honoring him or her with this special acknowledgment. Although a few names had been considered, at a class meeting the consensus was that we would not extol any one person, but rather that we would dedicate our yearbook to our parents. Not only was it a beautiful thought, but since I had been an English major in college, I was chosen to carry out the task, to recognize those who were truly instrumental in guiding and supporting us in all our academic ventures. A most wonderful, heart-warming assignment.

There is an ironic twist to the preceding narrative. When I applied for admission to Penn Dental I was an English major at Tufts College in Medford Massachusetts.. Since dentistry was my first career choice, I took many more than the required pre-dental courses, but I enjoyed literature and creative writing, and even had an image of myself as a college professor tucked away in a corner of my mind. It was my beloved cousin, Dr Sidney Shernan, who had implanted in me (pun intended) a desire to pursue what became my eventual profession. He let me shadow him at work occasionally, and showed me that dentistry was exciting, for it involved a unique combination of clinical skills guided by scientifically based procedures, all modified by an artistic bent and coupled with building pleasant inter-personal relationships. The result was that I was a bit of an anomaly. I had majored in English, rather than the usual chemistry/biology concentrations that pre-dental as well as pre-medical students usually chose to pursue in their undergraduate studies. One of my three interviewers for admission to Penn was the Dean emeritus. As we chatted he glanced at my record, and with a bit of whimsy said, "an English major! You can not only read but can write complete sentences?" Before I could think of an appropriate response he informed me that as far as he was concerned I would be accepted. And now, exactly sixty years later, I take pen in hand and write complete sentences.

UNITED STATES ARMY

August 1961. Goodbye to my life in Philadelphia. Back home in Boston for a brief visit with friends and family, then on to the next phase of my venture here on this planet, that of an officer and a gentleman. I felt a surge of pride as I put on my freshly-pressed Army uniform, crisp and dapper, complete with the shiny silver bars of a first lieutenant on each shoulder. After one more admiring glance in the mirror, I got into my little red Volkswagen bug and set off on the 2043 mile trip to San Antonio Texas, to report for active duty. My first assignment was six weeks of training at Student Detachment, Medical Field Service School, Brooke Army Medical Center, Ft. Sam Houston, Texas.

Today that trip, per computer inquiry, would take 37 hours, or one day plus seven hours of driving time. My trip took five days. The interstate highway system was just in its beginning stage of construction, and although there were a few turnpikes scattered around the country, most automobile travel was on two-lane highways. And personal computers with the capacity to plan and suggest the best routes were non-existent. So I unfolded a large map of the United States (available then at most local gasoline stations), and with crayon in hand, drew a line along a route that appeared to be the most efficient. A real pioneer! Ironically, it turned out to be a delightful venture, because it took me through so many small towns and cities that I saw a section of the country as a large panoramic view. The trip was quite interesting, for I could experience regional and social diversity as I stopped along the way both to eat and sleep in local establishments.

My journey took me through Philadelphia, so I stayed overnight with friends. In the morning I headed out for a tour of a country that I had not seen before. I just had to follow the crayon line on the map. It was exciting, for every bend in the road produced a new image. My first exposure to a life-style with which I was not familiar took place in Virginia. It was a hot afternoon, and I spotted a small diner up ahead that looked a fine place to stop for lunch. I drove into the parking lot which was alongside the building, got out, and standing tall with the perfect posture befitting an Army officer, headed for the entrance. As I approached the door I stopped quickly. Fastened inside the front window was a large menacing-looking sign inscribed with huge letters that proclaimed "WHITES ONLY." The sign appeared so foreboding that I actually stopped for a moment, read it again, and had to reassure myself that I would be allowed to enter. My first jolting experience south of the Mason-Dixon line. At that moment I realized that I was about to enter a world that I knew about only from books, magazines, newspapers, and Hollywood and radio depictions. I found myself suddenly looking forward to my new adventure. The next two years of my life would be quite different from any two that I had known before.

The line on the map then continued southward to Durham NC, where I treated myself to a brief tour of the Duke University campus. As I wended in a southwest direction, many hours later I found myself in rural Alabama, about 50 miles north of the Florida border, approaching a small town called Brewton. Since evening was quickly approaching and I was growing tired, I chose to make that my next stop. As I checked in to the local motel I noticed a strange, acrid odor in the air. It was as pervasive as it was annoying. The clerk informed me that we were a few miles away from a paper mill, and that after a while I would "get used to the smell." OK. Just another experience. There were treats for all of my senses.

The next morning I was determined to make as much progress as possible, so that the day would end with what would become my last stopover. As I drove through the outskirts of New Orleans the highway crossed over the Mississippi River on a huge, majestic, gracefully arching bridge that had been built, of course, by Huey Long. The scene was magnificent, and I remember writing home about the moment, saying that the grandeur of the structure appeared to reflect the majesty of the river over which it crossed. The view from the center of the span, up and down river, was stunning. I felt a sudden inner surge of patriotism. To me the Statue of Liberty and the Mississippi River were the two most powerful symbols of this great country. And now I had seen both. What made the moment even more exhilarating was that I witnessed the second one while wearing the uniform of the Army of the United States.

I had a placid feeling as I continued on westward, and came to my last layover, Opelousas Louisiana, a quaint town where I enjoyed a supper of roast chicken with dirty rice, a traditional Cajun and Creole dish. The white rice gets its "dirty" color from being cooked with small pieces of chicken liver or giblets as the juices from the roasting chicken drip into the mixture. Different, and very tasty. Next day, next stop, Fort Sam Houston, Texas. I was in the Army. What a feeling of pride as I drove to the main gate and presented my travel orders to the MP on duty. As I returned his salute I knew that I had just left my civilian life behind.

The Korean War had ended less than a decade before my graduation, but the cold war was always in the foreground, and there were many unsettling world events occurring in 1961. The Berlin wall was built, and a country called Vietnam was appearing daily in the news, with a few thousand "military advisors" having been sent to help, whatever that meant. The plane carrying United Nations Secretary General Dag Hammarskjold crashed in Northern Rhodesia, in what some people claimed was a result of an attack by another aircraft. These were troubling times. Military conscription had not yet ended, so that possibility still existed. To protect themselves, many dental and medical students opted to fulfill their military requirement upon graduation, by joining army or navy reserve units in their junior year of school. Commissioned as a second lieutenant in the United States Army Reserve, I was assigned to the 361st General Hospital. We were involved in a program that guaranteed us a commission as a first lieutenant and an active duty assignment upon graduation. The offer was eagerly accepted for two reasons: by completing a tour of active duty we could then establish a private practice without the possibility of interruption later by a draft call, and the service time would provide an internship setting where we could refine our clinical skills and learn to practice more efficiently.

There were further advantages to the post-graduation military experience. We would be granted administrative leave to attend courses, and by forming study groups we would create an on-going learning environment with our young and eager colleagues. Additionally, we would be promoted to the rank of captain after one year. And as a bonus, as we were now earning money we could pay off our school loans. I could also pay off the balance owed on my new Volkswagen, at $48 per month! I was so elated with my new status in life that when I paid my monthly Esso credit card bill, about $3.90 (gasoline cost 27.9 cents per gallon and my Beetle averaged about 35 miles per gallon) I would write "Dr. Bernard G. Park" on the back flap of the payment envelope. It was as though some 19 year old clerk in Raleigh, North Carolina would be impressed when she opened the letter to record the payment.

Now I was a soldier! As a youngster growing up in Roxbury Massachusetts during World War II, I can recall the swell of patriotism that was ever-present during my early school years. Pride in our military was heightened by the annual Armistice Day (now called Veterans' Day) parades in downtown Boston, with their display of tanks, artillery, plus the seemingly endless columns of sharply dressed soldiers marching erect with their rifles carried smartly over their shoulders. Mix in an abundance of John Wayne movies plus a constant flow of patriotic melodies (Praise the Lord and Pass the Ammunition; Comin' in on a Wing and a Prayer), and stirring images (Rosie the Riveter; flag raising on Iwo Jima), and you have the genesis of an eager desire to serve onetime in the military.

That was the background for anticipation of my first assignment, Medical Field Service School at Ft. Sam Houston in San Antonio Texas. It was a six week tour where we would be immersed in courses detailing military code of conduct, regulations, weapons use, including a week in the field at nearby Camp Bullis, practicing marksmanship on the rifle range, grenade throwing, triage, disaster, and evacuation drills. And then there was the famous infiltration course, recalled fondly by any former dogface who spent that day in fatigues crawling across a rocky field, sliding under barbed wire fences, while machine guns fired over our heads, and with carefully placed explosives, simulating a battlefield environment, detonating every few moments. A few of my cohorts were skeptical, saying that it would only be an exercise, and that the guns would certainly be shooting blanks, only for effect. Since we were not combat troops, the Army would never take a chance with the possibility of an accident jeopardizing the lives of medical officers! Enter reality. As we began our night maneuver, with the sound of several guns firing overhead, the white blur of tracer bullets could be seen illuminating the path of fire. One or two seconds later a terrifying shriek was heard above the clatter: "Holy shit. They are shooting real bullets!"

Ft Polk Louisiana was my permanent assignment. It had been active during World War II, then closed, re-opened for the Korean War, closed again, and had a grand re-opening when the Berlin wall went up and the cold war began to heat up. My original orders were to Ft Benning Georgia, my furniture was shipped to Ft Benning while I was at Ft Sam Houston. Then came the order change, and at the end of my tour at Ft Sam I was re-united with my furniture in Leesville Louisiana, my new home. For a lad who grew up in Boston and spent four school years in Philadelphia, my new town of 4689 people in the southwestern part of that state, eight miles from the Texas border, and with several dirt roads and a railroad track running through the center, was certainly going to be a novel experience. I knew I was living in the deep South when I first saw the sign on the highway that just skirted above Leesville that read "Natchez Mississippi... North."

The first time I placed a call to my mother in Boston I chuckled to myself when the local long distance operator asked "how do you spell the name of that town?" So many quaint regional expressions fascinated me at first, but soon became familiar. Once at a service station the attendant came to my car to inquire as to whether anyone was taking care of me, by asking, "you done been got?" It took me a few moments to figure that one out. If something was very good it was proclaimed to be "much mo' better." When in a conversation I was asked to ignore a statement or disregard a comment, the person would often tell me to "pay me no mind." If, in a discussion, I stated that something was possible, the local equivalent was, "it might could be." Perhaps the most colorful phrasing was the response that I got when I announced to a female clinic employee that my wife was pregnant: "Well the field's been plowed and the seed's been planted."

My house was a small two-bedroom ranch style on a dirt road. It had a carport, which once provided shade from the sun for a rattlesnake that hid behind a metal storage bin. I flushed him out by banging a rake against the side of the cabinet. I was than able to pin him down and finish the task with a machete that had been given to me months before by a neighbor. And then I was told that snakes travel in pairs in the spring, and that it would be a good idea to try to find its mate. So I spent the evening walking about the area searching, with a rake, flashlight, machete, and my dog beside me. Never found the other.

We had been briefed by the army on the dangerous critters indigenous to that locale, mainly rattlesnakes, water moccasins, coral snakes, and scorpions. I asked my neighbor if a scorpion's sting could be fatal. His answer was classic rural Louisiana. In a soft, slow drawl he said, "if you was bitten by a scorpion it wouldn't kill ya, but it would hoit so much you'd wish you was dead." As fate would have it I did spot a scorpion in the house a few months later. Remembering his words, I put on leather gloves, and made a king-sized wad of paper towels soaked in water. I got him on the first try. Every new experience was exciting, some a bit more than others!

Dialectical nuances and malapropisms were commonplace and although a bit different were easily understood. For example, one morning in the clinic a young recruit sat down in my chair and handed me his sick call slip. His sergeant had issued it, and had authorized him to go "to the dinil clinic." And I knew what the sweet little cleaning lady meant when she told me that she was listening to the radio and "the weatherman convicted heavy rain." However, my two years in Leesville had an effect which I could not have forecast. After twenty six years of living in big cities, I felt that the pace of small-town rural life would add more time to one's existence, a major factor that later led me to settle in Colchester Connecticut, population 5300.

I was an army dentist! Our detachment was comprised of fourteen newly minted dental graduates, plus a reserve medical service unit that had been called back to active duty and was charged with providing administrative support. They were to serve only a short time, until regular army officers could be assigned. As a result, we young'uns were given free reign in many areas. We were diligent in our work, trying to hone our skills. We formed study groups for discussion of current dental literature and to exchange ideas. We were enthusiastic about providing the best care that we could. And in short time we even learned the legendary army game that could make our lives a bit more comfortable. Supply sergeants were an elite group, and occasionally were given preference for appointments in exchange for field jackets, frozen steaks, copper tubing for home-made tv antennas, tools for personal use and jeeps to run errands.

Wheeling and dealing was often coupled with creative arrangements to achieve amenities and gain. But sometimes schemes can backfire. I cite one glowing (pun intended) example. Having been appointed x-ray safety officer, I was in charge of distributing and collecting radiation monitoring badges, as well as keeping a log of an individual's exposure time. One young private soon realized that if his report indicated that his readings were approaching an unsafe level he would be relieved of his disliked assignment of taking xrays. So one day he apparently held his badge under the x-ray head long enough (so he thought) to over-expose it and thus boost his numbers. When the report came back flagged with a red arrow I knew what had happened. His sudden dangerously high reading could not have been the result of his daily work schedule. He went from taking x-rays to peeling potatoes.

But my fun really began when I was appointed dental supply officer. Sometimes the Army method of operation produced baffling results .On occasion I could document duplication of effort, or wasted effort, and sometimes I witnessed duplication of wasted effort. A simple example will serve to illustrate. Each army unit had an inventory log, a manual (great army word) that listed every piece of equipment for every type of unit, from rifles for an infantry company, to pots and pans in the mess hall. Our dental manifest did not include a small hot bead sterilizer, a fairly new item that was used when performing root canals. It was a "nonstandard item". To obtain such an item required authorization for purchase, and had to be signed by the commanding officer. When I explained the need to the colonel and told him that the item could be purchased from a dental supply company in Shreveport, Louisiana for $60, I was informed that there was a specific protocol that I had to follow. Since the word "sterilizer" appears in the equipment list for hospitals, I had to requisition one from the medical corps. If, upon arrival, it was determined that it would not suit our needs, I could refuse to accept it and only then would I be authorized to complete the purchase from a civilian vendor. I filled out the paperwork (in triplicate) and a few days later a very large bacterial sterilizer was delivered to my clinic. It was the size of a small refrigerator and without doubt unsuitable for our needs. The one I wanted was small enough to be carried in the palm of one's hand. So I played the game. I filled out the proper form (in triplicate) and created a narrative explaining why the equipment could not be used in our clinic. And only then was my original request honored.

And then there was the Park Rating System. Since I was the dental supply officer I was told that an annual personnel evaluation had to be generated for each enlisted man in the dental supply unit. That was not a problem, but I was also informed that anyone receiving a low rating would require remediation, and that I would be in charge of retraining if that was required. Great! So I devised my own grading system: if a soldier showed up on time every day and appeared to be working, his rating was Excellent. If he worked fairly well and was a non-complainer, his rating was More Excellent. If he was a good worker and a self-starter, his rating was Most Excellent. Nobody ever needed help and tutoring! One time a conscientious objector who had been assigned to a rifle company but had asked to be transferred out because of his religious belief was attached to my unit. When evaluation time came around I asked the colonel if I should skip this new person, since he had been with us only a few weeks. I was ordered to use my judgment and appraise his performance as though he had been here for a year. By using my intuition and imagination as a guide to observation and evaluation, the soldier was deemed to be Excellent.. Sometimes the army's rules and regulations force a person to create a different path to make life a bit more rational. My system worked. It was not a deception or a misrepresentation. After all, evaluation is subjective, and affected by personal views and attitudes. I am often guided by the advice given by Ralph Waldo Emerson so long ago: "Simplify, simplify." And so I did.

Every detachment on every army post is subject to an annual IG inspection. The inspector general examines everything from administrative record keeping to unit cleanliness, plus adherence to the afore-mentioned equipment manual. Since Fort Polk had been opened and closed three times to accommodate a few wars, there was a small accumulation of extra dental equipment that we had found scattered about the clinics, such as articulators, extraction forceps,and dental lamps. When I asked the colonel for suggestions, since an IG inspector might question the existence of excess paraphernalia which would blemish our report, I was instructed to put them in a few boxes and take them to the dump. Although they were useful, their presence was not authorized. The reason sounded valid, but to throw them away seemed illogical. I had a better idea. One of my friends in signal corps sent over a pick-up truck. We loaded the items onto the vehicle and covered them with a tarpaulin. They spent four days hidden behind a garage. Everything was then returned to its former place as soon as the all-clear signal sounded. I never mentioned this to the colonel, for in reality I had actually disobeyed an order. But he was pleased with the IG report. We salvaged usable equipment. The inspection went well. Everybody was happy. The colonel never noticed, or even cared. Army logic at work.

Trading services for supplies and vice versa is a well-established tradition in all branches of the military, and is especially suited to the Army, with its many different types of units scattered over miles of specifically designated areas. The supply sergeants have been quite popular throughout military history, and are sometimes lovingly caricatured in movies and on television as skillful manipulators. My first encounter with this tradition occurred when one such non-com needed dental work but wanted to schedule his appointments at hours that were for him more convenient, a word not usually associated with military agendas.. He was entitled to have the necessary procedures performed so there was nothing illegal about arranging his visits at the specific times which he requested, and the field jacket that he gave me was Army issue, although not in the equipment inventory for dental officers. And it lasted for many years after I had returned to civilian life. There are not many uniform items that one can wear after leaving the service.

That was a simple swap. The television antenna required more complex manipulation. One of my signal corps officer friends had broken a very large filling on an upper molar. Replacing it with silver amalgam was the indicated and approved (translated: expected) treatment, but the ideal method of restoration, and one that would be considered in private practice, would be to replace it with a gold crown. However, that required documentation in order to secure permission to perform a "non-standard" procedure, so designated by the cost of the material plus the extra time involved. My request, complete with the necessary x-rays, was accompanied by a voluminous report that I generated to be so verbose and technically complete that I knew it would probably be skimmed over and approved without any request for further information.

And so he got his crown, and now wanted to re-pay me. A method quickly surfaced. I had recently purchased a large black and white tv set, but the indoor rabbit-ears that sat on top of the unit provided very poor reception. The nearest large city that had a tv station was Alexandria, about 50 miles away, so my channel selection was not only limited but the incoming signal was also quite weak. Using his communication skills and knowledge of broadcast bands, my patient constructed a large outdoor antenna, fabricating it with copper tubing and steel rods. He explained how he had measured the transmission wave lengths and then formed the components by bending and shaping the elements so that it would function at an estimated maximum efficiency. It was quite large, measuring about five feet across. In order to install it I attached the mast to a long bamboo pole, and fastened the device to a tree that was just outside the living room window. Rotating the unit slowly until I located the perfect direction, I then secured everything with duct tape. All went well. I could watch my favorite programs without having the picture disappear from the screen, and he was able to eat without worrying about his molar breaking again.

Adherence to rules and regulations form the framework for military life, but also provide a backdrop for the enterprising who either whimsically or with definite purpose attempt to alter them for personal gain or convenience. The regular clinic day ended at 1630 hours (4:30 p.m.), at the same time that many hundreds of clerical and support personnel would come streaming out of their nearby buildings and begin to leave the post. One of my colleagues had been in private practice for five years when his reserve unit was called to active duty at the time of the Cuban missile crisis.

He was an excellent practitioner, and his speed and skill outpaced our group of professional neophytes. Since he had joined us about a year after Ft. Polk re-opened, local housing was a problem, so he and his family rented an apartment outside of Alexandria Louisiana, about 50 miles away. In addition to the long commute, he found himself enmeshed In the traffic snarl that clogged the gate that he had to use to get to the highway. So he gave himself permission to leave fifteen minutes early each day. When the colonel discovered his new schedule, he was informed that in no way could he depart before the prescribed time, since that had been established by command. He tried to justify his reason. Since his daily production was much more than was expected (we had a daily procedure goal), the fifteen minutes were certainly more than off-set by his clinical prowess. He was a fast worker. However, the rule book does not have a section on logic! So to conform to regulations, he now did stay until the closing bell, but to satisfy himself he slowed down his patient load so that he was now performing the accepted minimum number of procedures. The colonel was happy. Everything was being done by the book! Illogical? Catch 22.

The clinic was a place where rules and protocol sometimes hindered the establishment of good doctor/patient relations. In addition to the regular dental chair configuration, there was a separate emergency section which serviced the patients who reported on sick call, plus a separate room where the oral surgeons performed their tasks. Since I had gone to Penn Dental where Dr Louis Grossman, the acclaimed "father of modern endodontics" taught, I was appointed chief of that specialty. However, I had not received training in surgical endodontics, for that aspect of the specialty was taught in the graduate dental program. Despite that, the colonel said that my responsibility covered all aspects of root canal therapy, both surgical and non-surgical. I performed my first apicoectomy (a procedure that involves flapping the tissue and removing the apex of the tooth) the morning after I read everything I could find about that procedure. On-the-job training at a high level.

So I was also the endodontic consultant. One morning a young recruit had presented for sick call, complaining of severe pain in a lower front tooth. My colleague, who had first examined him, had painted gentian violet around his mouth to sterilize the area before he would begin to diagnose the problem. He then determined that the young man required root canal treatment, so he was brought over to me. When I explained the procedure, he balked at treatment, opting rather to have the tooth extracted. The dental IQ of Fort Polk basic training recruits was a bit low. Many had never received dental care other than in emergency situations. Further explanation produced no results, so I had my assistant escort him to the oral surgery section. About five minutes later one of the oral surgeons came over to me and said, "you know that kid with the purple lips? He was seen by two of you before he came to me. He just wanted it extracted. So I took the tooth out. But I have a question to ask. Did anybody give him any anesthesia along the way?" The young soldier's tooth was not numb, but just sat through the procedure without a word or a complaint. Somehow communication was lost in that clinical situation. Unfortunately the structured environment with its ever-present background of rules and regulations can add just a touch of confusion and de-personalization.

I have often stated my impression that the last vestige of royalty in this country was in the military officer corps. The only two brick buildings at Fort Polk were a movie theater and the officers' club. The automobile bumper stickers which were required to drive on-post were color coded, red for enlisted personnel and blue for officers, meriting a salute from the MP at the gate as I drove through. There was a separate officers' latrine in each clinic. A person's rank was easily identified, and military protocol established a code of conduct in every aspect of daily life, from the arrangement as two or more of different grade walked together, to the proper way of speaking, and also responding. I paint this picture as prelude to an almost embarrassing situation. This could also add a bit more stress to the performance of dental procedures. I can illustrate with one precise example.

My patient on one morning was a two-star general. Imagine the pressure within me...perform a painless root canal with efficiency, as near to perfection as possible, while throttling any conversation that I usually initiated in order to help distract a patient, and merely let the general speak while I responded succinctly and with utmost respect. When I had finished I took a post-op x-ray. Endodontic radiography was difficult in 1962. There were no digital x-rays, and there were few effective cone-positioning devices. To obtain an image of the roots of an upper second molar was quite a task, and apparently I had just missed my target. As I waited for my assistant to return with the developed film I struggled to maintain a proper level of conversation with my patient, the general, who was obviously anxious to leave. When the young private returned and handed me the film he echoed the remark made by the technician who had emerged from the darkroom saying, "tell Captain Park to use his imagination." When the general looked at me quizzically I gasped for a breath of air, and then explained that the phrase was an inside joke, a way to say that all was well. The general thanked me as I removed his paper bib. As he walked out I used it to wipe the sweat off my brow.

The clinic administrators, lieutenant colonels, were an interesting group. A few could be considered to be quite professional, keeping up with the latest research, techniques and materials. Unfortunately one or two succumbed to the ennui which the routine of Army life could produce: secure salaries which often stifled ambition, officer rank that commanded respect and snappy salutes, access to the officers' club with its heavily-trafficked bar, regular hours with no weekend duty days. Complacency can set in. I can relate one incident that could be played out as a scene in a military-based movie. Early one morning, a young soldier was brought into the clinic for evaluation of dental/facial injuries. He had been on an infantry maneuver when he slipped in some mud which caused him to fall against the heavy steel bumper of a truck. It was more of a traumatic event and produced little bleeding other than that from a few scratches. Examination reveal no physical damage to either the teeth or supporting structures. I gave him an ice compress, instructed him regarding its use, and informed him that he may have some swelling later. I then sent him back to the field. He was not satisfied with my findings, insisting that he had broken his jaw. So I re-examined him and again sent him back to his duty post. Once more he disagreed, but now a bit more vocally. So I asked two of my colleagues to check his jaw. When they both confirmed my diagnosis, his disapproval of the exams became much louder. Just then the Lt. Colonel, a short, middle-aged, pot-bellied man, came ambling down the hall to see what had caused all the noise. I informed him of the situation. He spoke to the soldier in a gentle way, with his soft, soothing Southern accent re-assuring the lad that he would personally perform an exam. After about five seconds of palpating the upper and lower jaws, he reported that all was fine, nothing was broken, and that the soldier should return to his unit. As the Colonel went waddling back to his office one of my compadres told my patient that not only was his injury minor, but that he should feel privileged. "You better know your jaw's not broken. You just had a $650 exam. That was all the work that fat bastard has done all month."

As newly-minted dentists, we approached our work with enthusiasm, although sometimes with a bit of naivete regarding patient relations. Having completed a program of study that involved treating patients who had chosen a dental school clinic for many different reasons and were always receptive to our advice, we were now dealing with a quite different patient population, one that had been ordered to have dental exams and treatment. They had no choice. Since so many of the recruits had little or no regard for or experience with proper oral hygiene, patient education and awareness was nil. Also, since Ft. Polk was a basic training center, we faced a different group every ten weeks. Although we often attempted to explain the value and use of a toothbrush, we usually got a polite "yes sir", or just a blank stare. However, one of my experienced (label that 'recalled') colleagues devised his own method of demonstrating the importance of a clean mouth. When beginning to examine a patient who had obviously not brushed for days or possibly weeks, he would take a paper cup, pour in a bit of water, and hand it to the soldier, ordering him to put it into his mouth and swish it around. After ten seconds, he would instruct the man to spit it into the cup. Then he would hold the debris-laden mixture under the person's nose and order him to drink it. Of course the patient would demonstrate disgust, prompting the admonition, "if you can't put that back into your own mouth where it came from, how do you expect me to place my fingers there?" A bit crude, but an effective way to teach a lesson. Part of a boot camp experience.

As a Yankee from Boston living and working in a military installation in the deep South, I found that I was in a situation where I could experience first-hand the cultural differences that up until then I had only read about or seen depicted on film and television. I was now living in a town that was totally segregated. The movie house had a 'colored' entrance, the water fountain in the town square was marked 'white only'. Blacks lived in what everybody called 'niggerville', a section that was situated literally across the railroad tracks. My house was off-post, on a small street in the modest all-white residential area. It was obvious that if I was pleasant, polite, and never discussed politics or religion all would be fine. My neighbors were extremely friendly. I learned how to garden, go bass fishing at dawn, kill a rattlesnake as well as a scorpion, keep water moccasins away from my rowboat, boil crawfish, and drink white lightning.

The owner of the hardware store was also the popular mayor of the town. He always welcomed me, and provided advice on how to sink fenceposts to support a chicken wire garden fence, how to keep frogs and toads from settling in the back yard and attracting snakes, and how to fix a leaky faucet. As mayor, his store was often a gathering place for political cronies. And they always spoke freely and generally quite loud. I was meandering along the aisles one day when I overheard a local judge talking about a black man who had just been arrested and charged with theft. I froze when I heard him say to the mayor, "you bring that guilty bastard in and I"ll give him a fair trial." They had not seen me, for at that moment I happened to be standing behind a large stack of boxes. That one incident reminded me that I was living in rural Louisiana in 1962

However, it was a bit different in the clinic, where I was often entertained by my Southern compatriots with their latest President Kennedy jokes: "He gonna change the name of the Statue of Liberty. He gonna call it Our Lady of the Hahbah." "He gonna break Massachusetts up into two parts, High Mass and Low Mass." On occasion one of my Southern colleagues would begin to utter what appeared to be a contentious statement, but would catch himself and stop short. There were often subtle remarks, such as referring to the Civil War as the "War of Northern Aggression." But on the whole I must say that there was always an undertone of muffled respect. We would never agree on everything, so many things were better left unsaid. After all, we were all young, recent, eager to learn dental graduates who were serving our country. That was the great equalizer.

But I did have one shining moment when I could be critical, humorous, slightly sarcastic, and yet not cause any lasting or hurtful anger. The president of South Korea was a man named Chung-Hee Park, a leader who had just planned a visit to the White House. Since Park is a common Korean name, I have had many amusing moments in life as a result, such as receiving an invitation in the mail to an Asian holiday party at a casino, and a stream of advertising written in Korean from Korea Air Lines as well as long-distance telephone companies. But some karma must have been created so that his visit would present me with a golden opportunity. The Shreveport Times, a newspaper that was delivered to my house every morning, announced the visit with a headline that stated "Park To Ask Kennedy For Aid For South Korea." I could not resist. I cut out the headline, removed the word "Korea", and fastened the banner onto the clinic bulletin board. I told my Dixie brethren that I would do the best I could to improve their lot. It did bring about a round of smiles. I'm sure a few choice epithets were whispered about, but I had my 15 seconds of glory.

Army life provided me with many opportunities to enjoy my new situation more than I had ever imagined. I was developing professional competence while earning money (finally), and there were many amenities, such as the commissary and the PX, where shopping was less expensive than in the outside world. The United States was between wars, the Cuban missile crisis was over, and Vietnam was not yet a daily news item. One of my benefits was the availability of administrative leave to attend dental conferences anywhere in the country. Also, military travel was free. I would drive to Barksdale Air Force Base in Shreveport, Louisiana, a distance of 130 miles, and park my Volkswagon beetle behind the dental clinic. Then I would flag down a passing jeep to take me to base operations, where I would check the air traffic board which listed daily incoming and outgoing flights, sign on to a manifest of any flight of my choosing, space available, that would take me as close to the conference city as possible. I rode on many different types of military aircraft, and all at no cost. When flying on C47 transports, we had to wear parachutes during the entire trip, quite exciting for a Roxbury Kid who grew up watching movies showing John Wayne, Robert Mitchum, Clark Gable and Spencer Tracy winning World War II.

One trip was so memorable that I can recall it vividly to this day. I was heading for Boston, and was offered a ride on a cargo plane, a C 130 Globemaster. It was a huge four engine propellor-driven aircraft that had a cavernous cabin area, so large that one had to climb a long ladder to reach the cockpit. The pilot said that my security clearance was actually not high enough to allow me to be a passenger, but it was a night flight and I looked like a fine young, polite dental officer who would not create any difficulty or ask any questions. I was told that once we were airborne I could leave my bucket seat and climb up to join the crew for the flight. I did not question the discussion concerning the security issue because I was so happy just to be on board. They were going to Europe, but would stop at Dover Air Force Base in Delaware. I could easily catch a flight from there to the Boston area. But there was one stipulation: I was not to examine the cargo on board, nor ask any questions regarding the situation. Not a problem. I had a ride, and that was all I needed.

When I boarded I saw a massive canvas-covered mound, secured with dozens of ropes which were fastened in a manner to prevent any shifting during transport. I became curious, but remembering the pilot's instructions, I erased any thoughts about the cargo. As I buckled myself in, I heard the load roar as the engines were turned on, one by one. I then saw flashing red lights coming through the window. When I looked out I saw two fire engines flanking the aircraft. They accompanied us as we taxied to the runway, and continued alongside as we took off. It was too exciting to generate any nervousness within me, so I leaned back and relaxed until we were at cruising altitude, at which time the pilot called down and invited me to join them. While climbing the ladder to the cockpit I stifled any curiosity, I was not to ask questions. I was thrilled just to be up front, and enjoy the flight from a different perspective, one that few get to experience. The crew was quite friendly and interesting, and I spent five hours in fine conversation. They provided me with an Air Force box lunch which was comprised of the ubiquitous sandwich, apple, carton of milk and a cupcake. It was a repast that I never was able to replicate in future years, even tasting better to me than meals served on commercial flights in the first class cabin. To me it was like a scene out of a war movie.

When we approached the Dover area and were about to begin our descent I was asked to go back down to the cabin and buckle in for the landing. I did, and as I sat there staring at the canvas mountain I remembered my instructions, and resisted the urge to peek. When the plane began circling the field I looked out the window and saw a few fire engines flanking the runway, red lights flashing brilliantly in the warm Delaware summer night. As we landed I could see that the fire engines were in place at the end of the runway. When we touched down, they drove alongside, and came to a stop only when we did. Okay, that was enough to tempt even the most saintly individual! We had to taxi for a few minutes, so I had a chance. Unbuckling as fast as I could and hopping off the seat, I lifted up a section of the canvas at the bottom as high as I could and looked inside, It was an exhilarating sight. I found myself face to face with a huge mound of ordnance that was marked for delivery to Hahn Air Base in Germany. That explained the fire engines. As we left the plane I thanked to crew for the ride, and signaled a passing jeep to stop. Instead of having him take me to base operations so that I could hitch a ride for the final leg of my journey, I asked him drive me to the Greyhound Bus station. I had enough military flying for one day.

My last depiction of humorous recollections of army life involves an incident that is laughable now, but at the time that it occurred turned out not to be very funny, for it erased any thoughts that I may have held regarding a career in the U.S. Army Dental Corps. In my capacity as dental supply officer I often had discussions with the colonel about materials and equipment, usually on an informal basis. One morning I received a call at the clinic and was asked to report to detachment headquarters ASAP. How important could it be? Probably some small, in Army lingo 'chickenshit' problem. After I dismissed my patient, I took a slow, lazy walk, enjoying the early morning sun and the chirp of a few songbirds. As I entered the office and greeted his lieutenant, I casually asked what was going on that required my immediate presence. When I was told that the colonel was preparing court-martial papers, I asked "what's the poor bastard's name?" Imagine my shock when the reply was an abrupt "yours." The officer glanced aside, avoiding the astonished look on my face. I had no idea what was happening. Although I had sometimes slightly altered some rules and regulations playing the 'army game', there was never a transgression severe enough to warrant military discipline, let alone a court-martial. If convicted, the action would have severely and permanently affected and damaged my career.

On entering the room, I was ordered to stand at attention. The colonel had an angry, almost frightful look on his face. He placed a sheet of paper on the table in front of me, and turned it around so that I could read it. He pointed to a signature at the bottom of the note, and asked, "whose name is that?" "Yours

Colonel," I replied. "And whose signature is that?" "Mine sir," I replied without hesitation. "Then you are admitting that you forged my name, Captain?" "Yes sir," I replied. My response was strong, for at that moment I realized what was happening. Ft. Polk was located next to Leesville, a rural town, with many young families. The military was always open to public relations events that could make co-existence not only possible but also beneficial to all involved. One evening, while sitting at the officers' club bar with the colonel I had an idea that I shared with him. Since fluoride/vitamin therapy was fairly new and was becoming a standard of care, and since there were dozens of young mothers, both civilian and military, with scores of very young children, my suggestion was that we present a free clinic for any interested parents. We could provide a great service. Not only would I explain the benefits and application of fluoride as a dietary supplement, but we could distribute samples to those who wished to begin its use, and we could also stress the importance of consultation with their medical practitioners. The colonel was extremely pleased (the event might earn a citation for his military record). However, the tablets were a non-standard item (there's that term again) and would require the usual paperwork exercise, beginning with authorization from the commanding officer. "Do the paperwork Park, and just sign my name." I did as ordered, believing that we would be rendering a fine service to the community. However, I did not realize that my colonel was so drunk that he would forget, a moment that was reminiscent of a scene from a Charlie Chaplin movie. He totally forgot! That was why he became incensed when the requisition was placed in his inbox. He believed that I had forged his name. As I explained by reminding him what had transpired over a several glasses of whiskey, he seemed to remember. He did not say anything, and without any word of apology ripped up the paperwork and told me to go back to the clinic. Just a simple statement, "okay, go back to the clinic." My professional and personal life could have been damaged, but the incident was ended with just a rip of paper and a snappy salute.

At that moment I realized that private practice might just be the better choice.

So into my Volkswagon once more, and this time I will head north. And there is an ironic twist to the end of my active duty years. When my orders for return to civilian status were cut, they included a mileage allowance for travel home. The distance from Ft. Polk Louisiana to Mattapan Massachusetts was exactly 1776 miles. And every school child knows the significance of that number! But I must say that I did serve my six years (two on active duty and four in the reserves) with great pride in the Army and reverence for my country, and have always had great respect and admiration for all the service branches. That feeling is even stronger today.

PRIVATE PRACTICE IN COLCHESTER CONNECTICUT

As a person who had lived in big cities for the first twenty six years of his life, I surprised my family and friends by choosing to settle in a small town. Having passed both the Massachusetts and Connecticut state dental board examinations, I began to narrow down my possible practice locations. Of the two, Connecticut was a bit more appealing. I would be close enough to Boston to allow frequent visits and yet it was too far away to encourage frequent family interruptions. Anther factor that increased its desirability was the fact that the Connecticut dental examination was one of the most difficult for out-of-state candidates to pass at that time, and that state's license was therefore a bit more prestigious. Also, thanks to movies of the late'40s and early '50s, it was often portrayed as a state where the successful, the "beautiful" people lived. So the eastern half of the Nutmeg State seemed to be a logical choice. But where? How large a city? Perhaps a smaller town? One evening, while relaxing with my favorite libation, a tall glass with bourbon and three ice cubes, I realized that my life up to that moment had been played on a series of stages, several distinctively different locations, and that my more soul-relaxing episodes took place in Leesville Louisiana. I felt that the quieter pace would be more stimulating for me. Although that may sound a bit ironic, for attending a Red Sox game in Boston or the symphony in Philadelphia or a day at Mardi Gras jn New Orleans had always provided great enjoyment, I could be more natural and relaxed in a new semi-rural, less formal setting. A new locus for my psyche to plan the next stage of my trip on this planet. It may have been the result the new pleasures I had found in gardening, fishing, in being close to nature. I recalled the words of Henry David Thoreau: "Heaven is under our feet as well as over our heads."

I had contacted a representative from a dental supply company in New Haven, Connecticut, six months before I was scheduled to leave active duty. He provided me with a list of cities and towns where the ratio of dentists to residents was favorable for the establishment of a new practice. A logical point from which to begin. I took one week's leave and hitched a ride on a Military Air Transport plane to Boston, where I borrowed my sister Dorothy's car and then drove to New Haven. I was going town-shopping. The salesman and I drove through several of the areas that I had chosen as possible locations, stopping at a few town halls to speak to the clerks, asking questions about economic stability, social structures and population growth. There was very little warmth in some of their responses. That helped the process of elimination.

After three days of touring, we went to Colchester, where the town clerk was very encouraging, in fact almost enthusiastic about having a new dentist come to town. A small professional building had been opened a year before. The only tenant was a physician whose office occupied the left half of the first floor. The right side was being held, hopefully, for a dental office, another 600 square feet. There were only two other dentists, and the population was not only growing, but was about to increase dramatically as a new highway, Route 2, was approaching the area from Hartford. I did not know the meaning of the word epiphany, but I certainly felt it. However, again, having been the product of big cities, I began to feel an inner doubt about making a decision to bring my family, wife and one and 7/9th children, to a town of fewer than 5,000 people. The physician, Dr. Irwin Israel, was quite joyful about meeting his possible new neighbor. But, still feeling a bit of trepidation, I stated that I was concerned, because as we drove through the town I saw very few people. His nurse Sophie then said the six words that finalized my decision: "Open your office. They'll find you."

So I opened my office. And indeed they did begin to find me. Practice growth was slow at first, but began to increase at a steady pace. Then, three months later, I needed and was able to hire my first dental assistant, paying her the $50 per week which was about average at the time and was also the salary she had requested. Rent, dental equipment and supply payments, telephone, electricity, and now a salary! Too serious a situation in which to interject any humor, the least important part of my approach to practice at that time. Dentistry was a dignified business. My focus was on professionalism, and I was always concerned with saying the right words at the right time and in the right tone. Not an attitude of aloofness, but more of a protective mechanism. There were no instructors around to summon for help. Oh how I missed them now!

I quickly adapted to and enjoyed the pace of a small town in a rural part of the state. At first I was subjected to many questions from family members who found it hard to believe that a kid who grew up in a big city could so easily become acclimated to a quieter and, to them, less exciting lifestyle. When asked by my big city brethren just how small a town was Colchester, I developed a comical litany to counter their mocking inquisitiveness:

The town is so small that one day I plugged in my toaster and the street light went out.

The town is so small that the traffic cops hide behind each other.

The town is so small that the Howard Johnson's has only seven flavors.

The town is so small that the zip code has only four numbers.

The town is so small the entering and leaving signs are on the same pole.

The New Year's baby was born in May.

The local phone book has only one yellow page.

And my favorite: it's so small that it has a constant population. Every time a a baby is born somebody leaves town.

Small town medical and dental practices in the early 1960's offered an opportunity for professional courtesy to exist. Before the insurance companies became dictators of treatment and the federal government created a multitude of restrictive acts and regulations, the atmosphere for mutual care was prevalent. I provided dental services for my neighbor, Dr. Israel and his family, and he took care of our medical needs, including the delivery of two of my three children. One morning, as I lay on his examining table for my annual physical, he informed me that the next step was a test for glaucoma. The instrument used in those days was primitive compared with the digital techniques available today. The device was called a tonometer, and consisted of a bell-shaped instrument that the examiner would place on the surface of an open eye, and although it remained in place for only a second or two, it was an ordeal for a person like myself who was so sensitive that he could not even wear contact lenses. I squirmed around a bit, and implored him to please skip that part of my exam. I was only 30 years old. What could be wrong with my eyes? With a wry smile on his face he rejected my plea. "Remember the root canal you performed on me a few months ago?" I knew what was coming next. "I don't want to hear any complaints from you."

My good fortune in my new place in life continued as I began to develop a nice relationship with my landlord, Dave Flom. A native New Yorker, Dave had settled in Colchester when he married a local girl. Although to a great degree he was self-educated, he saw the potential impact of growth in the area as the state of Connecticut was building a major highway from Hartford through Colchester, which would link up with other highways and interstates. He went from being a delicatessen-counter operative to a real estate developer, and became quite successful. Although short in stature, he was great in his ability to use his innate intelligence in many creative ways. And he had a masterful sense of humor. Dave would stop by every few days to see if anything needed his attention. He owned two cars. One was a ten year old, unwashed Plymouth sedan with a dented fender, which he explained was "my rent-collecting car." The other was an elegant late model Chrysler, his family vehicle. His kindness was a buffer during my first financially difficult year of practice. One time I was five months behind in my rent. When I began to offer an apology he said, indicating no concern, that he was unaware of it, for "Molly handles the books." He was not unaware. He was being good-hearted.

If I was having a bad day he would soften it with tales of his own feigned "misfortune" that always helped change my mood. Putting a forlorn look on his face, he would cite his own adversity with a comment like "with my luck, if they cut a woman in half, I would get the part that eats." Or a pseudo-lament, such as "my wife on a shopping spree in G.Fox department store in Hartford reminds me of Teddy Roosevelt rushing up San Juan Hill, holding a credit card high as one would hold a weapon, running through the store shouting 'charge'." Financially astute, he was my mentor in my early stock market ventures when I was able to begin investing. His advice was sometimes elementary, but nevertheless sage. "In the stock market, bulls make money, bears make money, but pigs go broke." One time a sarcastic friend of his derided him because Dave had invested quite a sum in one particular stock, and quickly realizing that it would not bring about the financial gain he had hoped for, sold it a short time later. Nevertheless, he still made a small profit. His response to his detractor was immediate, and quite logical: "If I told you that you could make two phone calls, one minute each and one week apart, and that I would pay you $75 for your effort, would you not do it?" Case closed.

Perhaps the finest example of Dave's cleverness was his ability to turn a complaint into a benefit. In January 1978 the roof of the Hartford Civic Center collapsed due to the weight of snow after a massive storm. The incident was also linked to some degree to possible faulty design. As my practice was growing and my staff expanding, Dave had constructed an extension to my office a few months before that unfortunate event, in the heat of summer. As cold weather settles in new construction tends to develop a bit of contraction. I had no knowledge of this, but evidently the metal beams that formed the roof of my new office wing began to shrink a bit slowly, causing a visible gap to appear all around the ceiling of my treatment rooms. I called Dave to come and assess the situation. Before he would offer the structural reason, he tossed it off with a wonderful example of his ability as a builder to minimize or shrug off any problems. "The Civic Center roof fell down; your roof goes up." Priceless! The next day he covered the gap with molding, and the problem was solved.

While a neophyte practitioner with a still youngish looking face, I should not have been taken aback when the five year old sitting in my chair glared at me as I was about to begin examining his teeth and asked me if I was old enough to be a dentist. Or when another child looked about as he was preparing to leave, and asked me where the lollipops were. I had to explain gently that the physician next door has the lollipops, but, even better, in my office I had a treasure chest from which he could pick out a few trinkets. The plastic whistles and Chinese finger traps were the big favorites. This was not a good time for a lecture on the evils of sugar! There were many delightful episodes with my mini-patients during my first few years of practice. Fluoridated toothpastes had been introduced in the mid 1950's, although the effectiveness of that additive would not be measurably apparent for a number of years. Dental caries was still very high in children .As a result, my schedule was overloaded with the little ones, and to a great extent because the other two dentists in town preferred to treat only adults .In my senior year of dental school we had a course in practice management that was 5% business, 5% psychology, and 90% useless. We were given a list of words that should never be used in a dental office, viz, hurt, pain, drill, etc. So I had to chuckle when in the midst of a procedure I asked a ten-year old "does this bother you?" and he replied, "no. It just hurts." A young stoic.

The innocence of youth combined with the effectiveness of advertising once led to a question from my five-year old daughter that had me fumbling for a satisfactory answer. Since dental caries was still rampant in many children, the reduction in the number of involved teeth was the main topic of the early commercials for Crest Toothpaste, the pioneer in that venture. And of course they targeted the mid-morning and early afternoon children's television shows. So when Glynis came running to me one day when I came home from work asking, "daddy, what's wrong with me? The girl on television uses Crest toothpaste, and has only one cavity. I use Crest, and when you checked my teeth you told me I have no cavities. What's wrong with me?" I had to choose words that would lead to a simplistic explanation of the relationship between the effectiveness of stannous fluoride and the desire of Procter and Gamble to recoup R&D money, and thus bring a smile to the faces of their stockholders. After all, they are in the smile business. She understood when I told her that, "that the little girl had six cavities the time before. And now that she has only one means the toothpaste is very good. And that's why she was happy."

Through the years much has been written about the inherent wisdom of children. For two decades on both radio and television, famed performer Art Linkletter featured a segment on his popular House Party broadcasts which was called "Kids Say the Darndest Things", on which he interviewed schoolchildren between the ages of five and ten. This segment of the program quickly became the most popular, for it revealed, sometimes with embarrassment, the honesty as well as the exuberance of the little ones. I could relate to that show quite easily, for I was once a player in a scenario that could have been a mini-episode on that show.. My patient was a nine year old boy who had been scheduled for a cleaning, examination and fluoride treatment, my task before I was able to employ a dental hygienist. Before I began, he pointed to a loose baby tooth, and asked if I would extract it. As I held the tooth between my thumb and forefinger, it was indeed almost ready to fall out by itself. But he did not want to wait for that event to happen. Again he asked me to remove it, and in such an innocent way that I could not refuse. I placed a bit of topical anesthetic on the gum tissue, and taking a cotton 2x2 gauze square I squeezed it over the tooth, which of course slid out quite easily. Then he asked me to check around to see if there were any more that were so loose that I might extract them "as long as I'm here." His interest in shedding baby teeth at that particular time prompted me to ask why he was so focused on rushing a natural occurrence. After swearing me to secrecy (he was nine years old!) he revealed that he had discovered a money making scheme. The Tooth Fairy would leave a dollar bill under his pillow and, to his good fortune, would not take the tooth. So he banked his windfall, and that same day he sold the tooth to a friend for a quarter, so his pal could place it under his own pillow and await the visit from his own mythical benefactor. That took place many decades ago, and the family eventually moved away. Although I lost track of my little budding entrepreneur, I have a feeling that he eventually went on to become the CEO of some Fortune 500 company.

One incident involving treatment of children saddened me a bit, and led to many hours of discussion with co-professionals regarding the potential pitfalls of the new thrust of governmental participation in social engineering. In 1964 the federal Head Start program was introduced to help communities meet the needs of disadvantaged pre-school children. So one day, per their agenda, the town of Colchester arranged a joint medical-dental morning, that allowed parents to bring their young offspring to Dr. Israel's medical office for a physical exam, and then they would escort them across the hall into my workplace for a comprehensive dental exam, all at no cost to them. My protocol had the parent sitting in the reception area (the term "waiting room" was a verbal no-no... one of the few things we were taught in the practice management course), so that the child would not be distracted from the task at hand and perhaps could also begin to develop a bit of self-reliance. That morning I had examined thirty children, and felt good about my participation. However, I quickly realized that a well-intentioned program placed a spotlight on the weakness of an attempt to legislate human behavior. Only two of the thirty parents had bothered to ask me about the condition of their child's mouth. So disheartening.

There was another physician in town, a general practitioner who had an office not far from mine. He was well established in his practice, and was anxious to offer me some practical advice, so he invited me to his home one evening for dinner and discussion. Experience had taught him, and he wanted to share with me, what he considered the most valuable lesson that I could be ever taught regarding building and maintaining a successful practice. It was a proven fact that patients would judge me by "the three A's: affability, availability, and ability, in that order." It took me a little while to appreciate and accept his philosophy, for my dental school training emphasized clinical excellence to a point where, as a product of rigid academic discipline, I operated with the A's in reverse order from day one.

Eventually, when having become more secure both in my practice and in my finances I could relax to the point where I did not doubt my ability, had always made myself available evenings and weekends for emergencies, even performing an extraction one Christmas morning, and would began to lighten up a bit in my conversations with patients. Years later, after the practice had grown to include two partners, three hygienists, five dental assistants and a cadre of secretaries, I began to incorporate humor into my daily routine. Patients expected to laugh during their treatment, and one even said that I was not a stand-up comedian only because I sat down when I worked. One new assistant, after a few days of sitting chairside with me, said at noon that she was going to lunch, and would "get some popcorn for the afternoon show."

I took advantage of every opportunity to bring a bit of levity to the patient's visit. If music entered into the conversation, we would often break into song. In my early years I had a few elderly individuals who would often reminisce about the "days when music was nicer." There were many choruses of World War I songs that we would harmonize together, "Pack Up Your Troubles In Your Old Kit Bag and Smile, Smile, Smile." It would help them to relax, so I often sang, tailoring the selection to the patient's age and preference. As an added measure, I have a dreadful monotone which would always provoke laughter. I owned a metal pitch pipe which had been given to me by a kindergarten teacher, so my routine began with me blowing a few notes, calling each one out first. After the laugher would subside I would always own up to my awareness of the fact that my voice was terrible. "My voice is so bad that at the Red Sox game last week, while we were singing 'Take Me Out To The Ball Game', 38,000 people at Fenway Park asked me to shut up." "My voice is so bad that after singing the National Anthem at a high school assembly, I was accused of being unpatriotic and was asked to leave." "It's so bad that I am off-key even when I lip-sync."

And the handwriting! I truly believe that poor penmanship is the result of years of scribbling lecture notes very fast in order to keep up with the material being presented. And also compounded by the many times I had to write in a darkened classroom, while slides of the material under consideration were being flashed onto a screen a slight distance away. I often related the story of my attempt to master the Palmer Method of penmanship when I was in the 8th grade. True story. At the end of the school year each member of the class then submitted a sample to a committee, and if the cursive script was acceptable, a certificate would be issued with the pupil's name emblazoned upon it. True. I was not awarded a certificate. True. I then wrote to the committee, complaining about their failure to reward my effort. They did not reply. They could not read my writing. Not true.

In the early years my practice grew rather rapidly because, as noted before, I was willing to incorporate children into my daily routine. Fluoride use was in its beginning stages, and the average child of six already had a few cavities in deciduous as well as permanent teeth. The other two dentists in Colchester neither wanted nor encouraged pedodontic patients, and since I made the little ones welcome, many of their parents also became patients. Despite being bitten on the fingers on two separate occasions during treatment, I enjoyed interacting with the mini-people. (Why did I just get a mental image of the opening of the old Lone Ranger Show where the voice-over says, "let us return to those thrilling days of yesteryear"?). What a joy it was to see them racing the toy box to get their promised reward for being good while I "fixed their teeth and gave them a movie-star smile."

Their innocence was in sharp contrast to a few adults who tested my endurance as well as my patience in the earlier years. One of my earliest encounters with difficulty in the financial aspect of the real dental world involved a patient who had just obtained a dental insurance plan from his employer, and who needed quite a bit of treatment. At that time dental insurance plans were just beginning to proliferate. Since I was not yet able to employ either a secretary or a business manager, I had to explain the benefits as well as the limitations of each program to each patient. Having informed this gentleman that his plan would cover only a portion of the expense, I proceeded with the necessary care. When completed, I submitted the paperwork to the insurance vendor, and in a few weeks received their allocated remittance. On billing the patient for the balance I expected payment, for I had explained his responsibility three or four times before initiating treatment Now I knew that I had not seen him at any of my Mensa meetings, but I was unprepared for his method of paying his share. He walked into my office one morning with another insurance claim form, and as he began to hand it to me he instructed me to "put down that you gave me a gold 'toot'." I looked at him in disbelief, and explained why that would not and should not and could not be done. Neither hearing nor even listening to me, he left the paper on my desk and, as he walked out, instructed me to "keep any overpayment." I never saw him again, but I realized that I had just purchased a mini-course in practice management.

Another enlightening moment occurred when a woman whose check had been returned for insufficient funds presented herself with her checkbook in hand and showed me the ledger page. The check should not have bounced, because according to her records there was enough money in her account. "The bank will realize their mistake." How do I explain the financial system to her? Another woman, when quoted the fee of $300 for a crown, opened her handbag and showed me three $100 bills with which she would pay the fee, but would release the funds only after the crown was cemented. Another gentleman, a self proclaimed expert on cost-effectiveness, asked why I charged so much for x-rays. He stated that he was a purchasing manager for Pratt and Whitney Aircraft and as such he knew the true cost of materials. Overcharging? His challenging, almost demeaning tone demanded a sarcastic response. "I'll tell you the price. They cost $2.95 for a box of twelve." When that brought a victorious smirk to his face I added, "but it took me four years and cost me $80,000 to learn how to use them." I never saw him again.

And then there was the crotchety, toothless, elder gentleman who presented for a denture consultation. After examining his ridges and their associated structures, I informed him that he was a good candidate for full dentures, and went on and quoted my fee. He then told me that he had a set of dentures at home, and he had paid quite a bit less just a few years ago. I did not comment on the fact that they were not in his mouth, but merely restated my fee, suggesting that perhaps he should seek another examination and financial discussion in another office. This may have inadvertently angered him a bit as he replied with a scowl, "and I suppose you have an easy payment plan for those big numbers of yours." I could not resist: "Yes I do. It's ten dollars down and the balance at 5 o'clock today." I never saw him again.

Another time I was presenting a treatment plan to a used car salesman who was not being very pleasant. Not only did he complain about the fees, but he questioned the quality of my work. Would I guarantee the success of my treatment? Would it last a lifetime? What if something had to be replaced? Who would be responsible? Remembering my experiences with used car dealers in my earlier years, and their policy of issuing thirty day or 300 mile warrantees, I offered a comparable (to me) policy. "Good for thirty years or thirty meals, whichever comes first." Obviously, he had no sense of humor. I smiled as he left without saying a word. I never saw him again. It took a few years of practice before I understood what my cousin Sidney had meant when he told me as I began to practice that "dentistry would be great if it were not for people."

Although my joy in treating children was a large factor in the early steady growth of my practice, it was full denture construction that quite often gave me the most satisfaction, for a number of reasons. First, the results were immediate, and always gratifying. There was always a challenge because this procedure involved a blending of artistic, scientific and, perhaps more important, psychological skills. Often I would invite a family member to join in the process, to help evaluate the production before it was finalized, and also to lessen the embarrassment which so many denture patients felt because of their condition. Adding to these elements was the alarming fact that in 1965 about 20% of the population of the United States was totally edentulous—missing all their teeth. And an equally large number of people were missing all the teeth in one arch, predominately the upper. It was before the effects of fluoride use could not only be measured but also incorporated into a meaningful prevention plan. And it was the beginning of an era when periodontics and endodontics were both on the cusp (pun intended) of an explosion of research and practical application that would make gum treatment and root canal therapy efficient as well as predictable operations. These procedures were now more and more being accepted and covered by the newly proliferating insurance plans. In addition, it would be a few decades before research concerning dental implants would provide a more predictable, comfortable and lasting result.

In dental school we were cautioned to be careful in all of our pre-treatment consultations that involved full and partial dentures. After performing a thorough examination of the mouth, focusing on the condition of the dental ridges, tongue size, inter-arch space, cheek tissue quality and structure, plus lip size and configuration, we had to be reassuring regarding our prognosis, but not so optimistic that we might convey an unintended impression (pun intended) that the result would be perfect. Dentures are quite different from any other type of replacement, for in function there are so many moving components: lower jaw, tongue, lips, saliva, cheek muscles, and even the soft palate. Many clinic instructors added bits of information and suggestions during our training period that made our task a bit easier, but there was one caveat that was often repeated as a red flag that might signal potential difficulty: if at all possible, do not attempt to treat a patient who comes into your office with the proverbial "bag of dentures." Unfortunately there exists a small number of patients who have visited several dental offices and have had more than one denture made, none of which were able to be worn without a bit of discomfort for any number of reasons. Technical problems can be identified and corrected, but patient over-expectation will always preclude a satisfying result. There is nothing like your own teeth!

So, despite knowing all of this, I could not resist a challenge. One sunshiny morning a rather pleasant looking woman in her early 50's had an appointment for a denture consultation. She was wearing both uppers and lowers, which she said just plain hurt all the time. With a bit of an effort, she then flashed a little smile so that I could see the cause of her complaint. They looked rather satisfactory, but they hurt when she ate. And then she opened her handbag and produced another set, which she said fit as comfortable as possible, but just looked awful in her mouth. She had complained to her two former dentists but was always told that "false teeth are at best a poor substitute for the real thing." She had disagreed, but to no avail. Could I help her? Quick evaluation revealed a fairly charming, nicely dressed person with a complaint that was quite plaintive, somewhat downcast and had just a hint of a challenge. I just had to proceed. Using caution before obligating myself, I inspected both sets of false teeth, and then turned to a very careful examination of her oral structures. "I'll give it a try." Her quick smile signaled understanding. The fates were also smiling. The result was gratifying. She could eat without discomfort, without trepidation, and her broad smile returned. And she was rather attractive.

The case was successful, but more so than I had realized. Since she was the only member of her family that I had treated, and my conversation with her was always guarded, I knew very little about her personal life beyond her dental experiences and expectations. I had accepted a challenge, and knew that it was a one time event, for she lived about thirty miles away. A few years later I received a letter from her. She wanted me to know that all was well and she was very grateful for the care we provided. And her life had changed. She was now living in California. She had divorced her husband, met a slightly younger man (I'm not sure of the true order of events), and was now remarried. And the best part was that not only does her new mate love her smile, he has no idea she is wearing dentures. That was the only time that I ignored a red flag .The challenge was too great, but I always enjoyed that aspect of dentistry. So easy to bring about nice changes to a person's appearance and self-esteem.

One of the learning experiences of a neophyte practitioner was to disregard the pandering use of the newly acquired title by merchants or vendors who invoked contrived flattery in an attempt to create a congenial setting for a sale or investment Their technique was to repeat the word "doctor" as often as they could in dealing with recent graduates, with the hope and belief that an inflated ego would lower sales resistance. I received a large dose of feigned respect and an encounter with a genuine huckster when I attended my first Connecticut State Dental Association's annual meeting in 1964. I was in the exhibitors' hall, standing next to a small gathering of dentists who were being given a presentation of a new impression material, I found myself almost in front of a table where a nattily-dressed vendor was taking orders for the Encyclopedia Americana. As the gentleman caught my eye he tried to engage me in conversation, despite my polite rejections, and my repeated saying that I was not interested in his wares. I was trying to learn about the dental material that was being presented in the booth next to him. Despite my obvious disinterest he continued his persistent, repeated, sales pitch that droned on with monotony.

"Doctor, you will find the encyclopedia quite useful, doctor." This annoyed me. But not only did he disregard my request to stop, he placed an order form on the table in front of me and said, "doctor, just sign here. If you are not satisfied, doctor, you can return the set." I could not resist the urge to be just as irritating. "You just want me to write my name?" I asked. "That's right doctor." So I took his pen and wrote the words "my name." As I pushed the contract toward him he muttered something unintelligible. I am sure he did not use the word "doctor".

Dentistry was undergoing great changes at that time. The introduction of high-speed, air driven, water cooled drills was a monumental event in the history of the profession. But it also produced a number of caveats, such as using care and judgment in evaluating new adjunct materials that manufacturers claimed would make the new technology even faster and safer. One time a sales representative for a dental supply house announced that he had a revolutionary new product that would solve a problem which was now occurring in dental practice. The high speed drill, which made cutting teeth much easier and faster, would often create a slurry of debris and water that would diminish the effectiveness of the dental mirror, requiring a break in the procedure to clear the surface. This was during the brief period before today's four-handed dentistry had evolved, where the dental assistant now sits beside the seated doctor and clears the visual field with a steady stream of water. His company was marketing a "spinning mirror," a device that attached to the dental unit's air compressive mechanism. The surface of the mirror would rotate at a moderate speed and thus cause any bits of junk to fly off by centrifugal force. Great idea in theory, but I asked him how it could be used with safety, for it might come into contact with the patient's soft tissues no matter how much caution was exercised. Also, using the dental mirror to retract a cheek or deflect a tongue was common during treatment. In fact it was almost a reflex action. A fast rotating surface would certainly bruise, and could even lacerate. He said he had no answer. I never saw either him or his invention again.

Practicing in a rural area often limits a general practitioner in his choice of specialists when referral of a patient is required. Sometimes the selection is influenced by the distance between the two offices. In my early years there were two oral surgeons in my greater area, with one being a bit closer than the other. Since they were equal in skill and experience, my preference was, on occasion, based upon the patient's comfort level in driving to either city. After a while I had a problem with one of my colleagues who was not proficient at communicating. Too many times he would forget to inform me of any treatment that he had rendered to my patient, and thus I was unaware of its result or of any possible complications. I would have to call his office and ask for a treatment summary. Whenever we met at local dental society meetings he would promise to be better at corresponding, but to no avail. This led to many embarrassing situations. As an example, when I would ask a patient on a recall appointment why the recommended treatment was not pursued, and the person would say that indeed my advice was followed and the surgeon had corrected the problem. Since there was no progress note in the record, I assumed that for any number of reasons my patient had chosen not to seek further care. There were so many situations like that, so I stopped sending referrals to that office. When the surgeon and I met again at a dental gathering, he would question the stoppage, and a few times he would say "let me hear from you." It became an annoyance. So one day I asked my secretary to call his office, get him to come to the phone, and just say "Dr Park says hello." He never spoke to me again.

As the practice and my confidence both continued to grow, I was feeling a bit more relaxed. I realized that one of the aspects of my work that prevented boredom was the fact that although I might perform the exact same procedure on five people in a row, they were actually five different procedures because of the differences, both physical and psychological, among the individuals. One morning I was taking upper and lower arch impressions for a man in the beginning of the process of full denture construction. The material in use at that time was a compound called alginate, one that had a putty-like consistency. When the loaded upper impression tray was placed in the mouth it filled most of the space, yet it allowed the patient to breathe slowly for the few minutes of setting time, obtaining most of the air through the nose. I had performed this procedure several times before, issuing the same instructions while holding the tray in place and reassuring each patient in a slow monotone that all was fine and that we were almost through. After about thirty seconds my patient began to laugh almost uncontrollably, even though his mouth was filled and he could not communicate. As a tear or two began to trickle down his cheek I said that we had to wait just a bit more before I could remove the finished impression. When we were done I wiped his lips and asked what could possibly have been so comical at that moment. He was sitting there with his mouth filled, his gag reflex barely stifled, breathing slowly through his nose, in essence trapped for a few minutes. "I had a great thought," he said. "Where can I get some of that stuff for my wife?" It was then that I wondered why the words fun or funny had never been included in my dental school curriculum.

Once a light moment had to be quickly aborted so that I could complete the procedure at hand. My patient was a very witty middle aged ex-New Yorker, a pleasant man who always had a contagious smile on his face and who took pleasure in any type of humor. I had just purchased a Jackie Mason cassette tape, a recording of his current hit Broadway show. When I finished anesthetizing the tooth du jour I offered to play the tape for him, so that we could both enjoy it as I worked. A few minutes later I had to turn off the sound system, for he was laughing so hard that I was afraid to continue for fear that I could cause damage. His mouth was a moving target. And although I performed my task in silence, I had to stop every minute or two as he would mumble a line from the show and begin laughing all over again. And there were actually tears in his eyes, and none were caused by any discomfort.

My new stereo system offered me a chance to score a one-time victory over a curmudgeon. Sidney was a pharmacist in town and was also my neighbor. Although he was overall a very pleasant person, he demonstrated at times that he could be quite set in his ways. Albeit not often argumentative, once his mind was made up about anything he disliked he would not listen to anyone's point of view. As a life-long and die-hard Red Sox fan I was fortunate to be able to attend about a dozen games a year. Since it took me an hour and a half to drive to the ballpark, my neighbor often found the opportunity to tell me that as far as he was concerned the whole matter was a waste of time and money. Baseball was a foolish sport. But one day I came upon an example that I believed would justify my passion. When Bartlett Giamatti resigned as president of Yale University to accept the position of Commissioner of Major League Baseball, I explained to my friend that when a man who is considered to be a nationally known Renaissance scholar leaves his exalted post in academia to become the head of a sport, that move by itself must speak well for baseball. His response was, as anticipated, negative. Not worthy of consideration or debate. Okay. No more discussion. He had the last word. He won, although by default.

Then came the wonderful afternoon when he was seated in my dental chair at the beginning of a long appointment. Having just installed my music system, I was excited about its potential for distraction and relaxation, and to make it even more enjoyable I always offered a choice of artist or genre or even song to every patient. This was something even he would enjoy. "What would you like to hear?" His reply, although not surprising, was not anticipated. "Nothing. I don't want music." I tried a few more times, but his response was always laconic and final. Suddenly I thought of a way to satisfy him while also winning the argument. "I'm going to play something," I said, and without looking to see his reaction I took the cassette head cleaning tape and slipped it into the stereo player. We both sat quietly as thirty seconds of silence emerged from the speakers. Without either of us uttering a word, I went back to work. Gratifying to me, and it also brought a little smile to his face.

In contrast to the congeniality of routine treatment situations, there were many instances when I had to respond to a question that was either borderline insensitive or an insult in thin disguise. Once an elderly gentleman had an abscessed wisdom tooth that had progressed to a point that his condition required treatment by an oral surgeon. Although I tried to explain the reason behind my decision, and even had to explain why various specialists existed, he continued to balk at having to travel twenty miles to another office. Finally he realized that he had no choice. With a stern look on his face, he arose from the dental chair as I handed him the referral slip and mumbled, "what ever happened to the dentist who did everything himself and never sent a patient to a specialist?" Although my answer may have been a bit smug, it was also immediate: "He had a heart attack." Another interesting moment occurred when Dr. Mike Babinski first joined the practice. Since Colchester was a multi-ethnic town, I should not have been surprised by the woman who wanted to know a bit more about him than had been presented in the press release that had announced his association with my office. When she asked in a rather demure way, "so tell me, what kind of a name is Babinski?" to which I just replied, "a last name." No further questions! The late actor Peter Ustinov once wrote that "comedy is simply a funny way of being serious."

With the growing belief that inter-personal relationships were just as important as clinical skills, I enrolled in a continuing education course at Tufts Dental School in Boston, in a subject that changed my approach to practice––transactional analysis. Briefly stated, it is a study of patterns of human interaction that identifies three ego states: parent (nurturing, controlling), adult (grown up), and child (playful, innocent), and also how they converse with each other. Not only is what is said important, but also how it is said. Communication can take place at any of three levels, or it can involve upward or downward movement between the parties. Complementary transactions take place when both people are on the same level. I can illustrate this by describing one of my pet peeves. The physician (I use that example because

I have found it to be the most frequent) who, in describing to a patient the nature of his or her problem, often uses the phrase, "you have what we call......" By this tone and word selection, "what we call," the doctor is placing himself or herself on a higher plane than the often already frightened patient, who certainly has none of the knowledge or training, and is therefore being talked to in a downward direction, e.g. parent to child. Not very comforting. It would be much better for the anxious patient if the conversation was more adult to adult, which could begin, "you have a condition known as...." And then to go on and explain in an understandable fashion what the problem is, and what is required for treatment. Although both parties may be on different social, educational and financial levels, the discussion would be on a more even keel. Without doubt a much easier, and also a kinder way to communicate.

Humanize the dialogue. As an example, every dentist asks everyone at least once every visit if he or she flosses. When my patient would begin to deliver an evasive answer (normal reaction, for very few people floss with regularity), I would soften any discomfort of the moment by recalling the story of a patient who reported that he flossed "religiously." My response was, "of course you do. Every Easter and Christmas." Then I would erase any possible further dismay by telling the patient to, "make flossing the second last thing to do before going to bed." And of course I would then be asked, "what's the last thing I should do?" "Shut off the light." More effective, I believe, than stating, "you have what we call incipient periodontal involvement, and I must impress upon you the need to floss at least once daily, but preferably twice, morning and night." At times even gentle sarcasm can be effective as well as acceptable: "You do not have to floss all your teeth, only the ones you want to keep." Lecture delivered with ease, and perhaps remembered a bit longer.

There were fortunately a few instances through the early years that taught or, even better, often reminded me that I would not always be in fluent connection with my patients. One incident in particular demonstrated how detached a person can be from what I observed to be the real world. It occurred the day when the annual town meeting was scheduled to be held in that same evening. On the agenda was the presentation of the education budget. Discussion would be held, and then the voters would either accept or reject the proposal .This was often a contentious event, when pro-education supporters tried to outnumber those who were bent only on keeping expenditures to a minimum, and who were not interested in the substance of the presentation. And here I was the Chairman of the Board of Education, who was at that moment inserting a denture for a man who often spoke very little. Midway through treatment he raised his hand to indicate that he had something to say. "There's a town meetin' tonight and you should go. They tryin' to push up our taxes, and we have to vote it down." Simplistic and conclusive. I thanked him for reminding me, and assured him I would be there. He was interested only in lowering his own town taxes, and was oblivious to the structure and elected officials of town government. It was then that I began to believe in parallel universes.

Education does not always involve institutions of higher learning. I learned a most valuable lesson in patient management and communication in a most casual way. It was during the Thanksgiving vacation in my first year at Penn. Not only was I anxious to see my friends and family, but was also most energized by the opportunity to visit my cousin Sidney's dental office. I was now on my way to a career in his respected field. He was not only my dentist, but also my role model. Sid had been a fighter pilot in World War II, and had an infectious zest for life. Having already been exposed to three months of professional schooling, I could now begin to relate to him as an equal, perhaps even incorporating a few dental terms into our conversation. I felt very proud of myself, and could not get to Malden Massachusetts fast enough.

With a sense of pride, and with his patient's permission, I looked on as he did his work. I noticed that he mixed the amalgam (silver plus mercury) for the filling with a small mortar and pestle. This had been the accepted method for generations, but now there was a mechanical mixer available that performed the same task in a matter of seconds. Wow. Something I could discuss with him as a co-professional! When he had completed his morning schedule we had a chance to discuss dentistry. When I asked why he did not upgrade his work with the new technique, he responded by giving me the greatest lesson I ever learned from either an instructor or a textbook or a colleague. "I know about the amalgamator, but I do not want one. I want to have the luxury of leaning against the wall as I mix the material, and enjoy the comfort of a few minutes of quiet conversation with my patient." Lesson not only learned, but one that became a guideline for patient relations during my half century of practice.

I always played background music. At first it was a radio, then came tapes, followed by compact discs, and now on to mp3 players. Progress in music recording grew as fast as did newer techniques in dentistry, and I could now tailor the music to the patient. I would always ask what kind of music he or she wanted to hear. So often the reply was, "play what you like," to which I always offered the same response: "No. The music is not for me. What do you want to hear? If you were not here I would not be here." That line formed the framework within which I practiced.

As years passed by I added many axioms, which I gleaned from many diverse sources. I incorporated them into what I often referred to as the Bernie Park book of guidelines for life One of my favorite gurus, the late Dr. Wayne Dyer, influenced me with his central thesis, that, "I am not a human being having a spiritual experience, but rather a spiritual being having a human experience." Realizing that we are all traveling together on this planet and during this same time, I always felt a strong kinship with my patients. He helped me refocus on life and reality when he wrote that, "if you change the way you look at things, the things you look at changes." This helped so many times. If I had a difficult moment I could shift my perspective and could begin to observe the scene through the patient's eyes, be it a financial matter or a failed root canal or even the first glimpse of a new, beautiful smile.

And an even more disparate source was a comedian, the late George Burns. At age 99, when asked the secret of his longevity, he said that it consisted of two principles. The first was "fall in love with your work,' and the second is, "you can't help getting older, but you don't have to get old." Simple, but very powerful. I truly enjoyed my dental practice, always looking forward to Monday mornings, a statement that always surprised many of my friends who had been involved in several other ways of earning a living. But at age 80 I changed careers and became an author, something I had long considered and which I made a personal pledge. For many, many years the words of Dr. Dyer which I had read decades ago almost haunted me, and became my next mission in life: "Don't die with your music still in you." And, after all, I had been an English major at Tufts.

The late pianist/humorist Victor Borge once wrote that "laughter is the closest distance between two people." Through much of our early history professional people, especially those in the health professions, were sometimes perceived and in movies were quite often portrayed as being a distinct group, somewhat detached and quite a bit distant. Neither a comfortable setting nor a pleasant atmosphere within which to provide care for people who were already ill at ease and were seeking both physical and emotional help and guidance. The very nature of dental treatment can create a threatening situation for a human being. The mouth is the instrument of verbal communication, a portal for the intake of sustenance as well as the major component of the breathing system. And as the dentist blocks part of this space, the patient is, for a brief period of time, unable to connect effectively with the outside world. One realizes that eating, drinking and even breathing may seem to be impaired. To help minimize the feeling of isolation, humor allows a person to participate in the treatment process. Reassurance from the dental team helps a bit, but it is the sound of laughter that makes the process a bit less threatening. And when the patient is able to join in the exchange everybody gains. The distance narrows just a bit.

As an example I cite the time when I was performing a comprehensive exam on a new patient, an elderly woman who appeared to be just a bit anxious. Before I began I told her that she would hear me calling out unfamiliar terms to my assistant Barbara, who was making notations in the patient's chart, but that when we were finished I would explain to her "in English" what my findings were and would suggest a treatment plan. Now I tend to be a bit verbose, always trying to be more conversational rather than clinical in my presentations, especially with new people. I could be a friend as well as their dentist. After a lengthy discussion I asked if she had any questions, saying that, "I sometimes talk a lot." Her white hair framed a warm smiling face, and with a bit of a twinkle in her eyes she replied, "I hadn't noticed." Gotcha. We became immediate friends. I always reminded her at subsequent visits through the years that the score that day was Dorothy 2 and Bernie 0. And she always appeared relaxed, sitting quietly in the chair, with a look on her face that seemed to be saying, "you don't know when I'll get you again."

Using my music-teachers pitch pipe and a kid's purple plastic microphone I discovered that when I sang as I worked many patients were both amused and distracted by my monotone and by my total inability to stay on key. I noticed that they changed their focus for a moment, and often began to relax. Most even laughed as I plodded through a song. One person tried to console me by stating that what I lacked in ability I made up in determination. Once, while administrating nitrous oxide at the beginning of a procedure I began to sing is a soft voice. My patient immediately said, "more gas! Please! I can still hear him." I believe the technique was proven effective by the gentleman who was moving from town and came in to say goodbye. He stated that he could not leave without thanking me for the care which he had received, and had to tell me that, "the only time you ever hurt me in the last twenty years was when you sang a song or told a bad joke."

Patients always felt free to engage in light-hearted humorous exchanges. A few were so good that they qualify for the Punsters Hall Of Shame. "I feel as though I'm at my proctologist's office...you are making me the butt of your jokes." Often they would begin a thread of related whimsical remarks. "You did not lose my records, you just rectum." "Play some nice music. My gynecologist's music annoyed me, but I did not want to stirrup any trouble. Would rather hear Urethra Franklin." And then there was the couple who had become recovering alcoholics dancing to their favorite tune: Liver Come Back To Me. Another duo were in the back seat of their car at the drive-in movie. The film was titled From Here To Maternity. And the laboratory animal that passed out. "His partner saved him by doing mouse to mouse resuscitation."

On occasion a medically-challenged patient would relax enough in the flow of wittiness to join in with an ironic comment about his condition. One fine gentleman, a patient of about forty years, had become afflicted with Parkinson's Disease and had regressed to a point where dental treatment was a challenge. He often apologized for the difficulty he was creating, but we always assured him that it was not really a problem because we were able to perform whatever procedures were necessary. One day, as Barbara had just seated him, he said that to make it a bit easier for us he had not taken any Viagra the evening before, because it just makes him shake harder. Any pity was quickly changed to admiration.

Many madcap melodies were composed on the spot in response to a patient's statement or to a question. For a fan of country and western music I sang a modified ditty: "Oh show me a home where the buffalo roam, and I'll show you a house that's a mess." When a parent asked about the possibility that dental x-rays might be harmful to her child, I sang my new version of an old song: "Wait 'till your son shines Nelly." And my modification of a once-popular romantic ballad: "I saw you last night and got that old filling." And, of course, when the two nearby gambling casinos opened for business, I would offer my Tony Bennett-like rendition of "Stranger With A Pair Of Dice." They may not have been memorable, but they certainly were note-worthy. (Pun intended."

As entertaining(?) as the lyrical license may have been as well as relaxing, my only attempt at impersonating a well-known actor fell flat one day. John Wayne's voice was well known, especially for his slow, often deliberate drawl. Once in a while I could come close to sounding like him for a moment or two. So one morning, after the patient was anesthetized and ready for Barbara and I to begin, I raised my right hand, extended my thumb, and pushed an imaginary cowboy hat further back onto my head, saying, very John Wayne-like, "Ok l i t t l e l a d y I g o t m e a t o o t h to f i l l ." It was actually pretty good, according to the two witnesses. However, later that day, when I attempted to duplicate my only successful impersonation I fell a bit short, for the patient looked at me and asked who the person was. "Why that was John Wayne, of course" I proclaimed. The response caught me off guard: "John Wayne the actor?" "No," I replied, "John Wayne my mother's butcher back in Boston." Rich Little did not have to worry about competition.

Many patients enjoyed an exchange of jokes as they were seated in the dental chair, so I would often let them begin the process. Responding to small talk with joshing was easy. When a patient would express dolefulness about becoming older, I would tell them that "age is relative...and I have some relatives who are aging me." If they complained about their misbehaving offspring, I would cite the maxim that "insanity is hereditary. You get it from your children." When a complaint about a spouse was the topic I would soften the discussion by reminding the complainer "there is a reason why there is a severe penalty for bigamy...you get two mothers-in-law." To the patient who was becoming both nervous and annoyed by the amount of time involved in the treatment, I would say in a soft and reassuring voice that the end of the procedure was approaching: "We are reaching the point where I can say to you, as the Wolfman said to Dracula, 'we are fiendish'." The irritability disappeared.

There were jokes that lent themselves to adding a bit of cheer to the patient. As practice management consultants and motivational gurus teach us, the most pleasant sound a person can hear is his or her own name. Carrying this a bit further I realized that not only the name, but also a recognition of a specific interest, be it golf, football, literature, movies, etc. provided a fertile field upon which I could plant a few seeds of comfort. Studies have shown that a very large number of patients evaluate a practitioner less by their perception of his or her knowledge and technical skill, but much more by their feeling of how much the doctor knows and cares about them. Finding common ground and directing the conversation toward the patient's hobby or pastime thus often helped to ease the tension of the moment. I would embellish any discussion of a patient's stated area of enjoyment with an appropriate witticism that zeroed in on their vocation, avocation, or any method for relaxation which they enjoyed. My list of favorites follows. They served well for decades:

> * Golfers: when a visibly upset golfer came into the 19th hole for a bit of after-game refreshment, he told of his terrible experience. Just as he was teeing off on the third hole, his golf partner suffered a massive heart attack. "That must have been awful," said a fellow player. "You don't know just how bad it was. Tee off, then drag old Charlie, putt, then drag old Charlie."

> * Literary types: the famous lexicographer Noah Webster was romping in bed with a lady friend when his wife happened to return home early. As she opened the door into the bedroom and looked in, she was startled. "Noah, I am surprised," she said. His response was quite precise. "No my dear. You are amazed. It is I who am surprised."

> * Political buffs: Ned and Jed were two elderly New Hampshire farmers who were attending their small-town's Fourth of July celebration. Standing

on the bunting-draped bandstand, the mayor was delivering his holiday oration. After speaking for about fifteen minutes, Ned, who was hard of hearing asked, "what's he talking about Jed?" The reply was succinct and accurate. "He ain't said yet."

* Teachers: in a sociology class the instructor was taking an informal poll regarding sexual activity. "How many of you have sex a couple of times a week?" A few hands were raised. "And how many of you have sex a few times a month?" More hands held up. "How many have sex a few times a year?" More hands shown. "And now a foolish question. Is there anyone who has sex only once a year?" "Yes, me, me," said a young man, jumping up and down as he waved his hand back and forth. "Did you hear my question? Only once a year?" "Yes, yes, once a year." "Then why are you so excited?" "Tonight's the night, tonight's the night."

* Football fanatics: it was opening day at the stadium, and returning season ticket holders greeted each other as they headed for their long-held seats, exchanging accounts about their activities during the six month break after the championship game. As one fan went to his seat, he was asked by his neighbors why he was alone, since his wife had always accompanied him in the past. When he told them that his wife had passed away, they were saddened, but wanted to know why he did not bring a friend or relative with him to the game. "Couldn't get anyone to come. They're all at the funeral."

*Clergymen: a man lived across the road from a Catholic cemetery. He was a bit of a loner, with only his beloved cat for company. Alas, one day his pet died. Since the man had often sat on his front porch in his comfortable rocking chair gazing across to the placid view of the burial ground, he had a strong desire to bury his feline friend there. He would take comfort in knowing that his long-time companion was somehow still nearby. When he approached the caretaker to discuss his wish, he was informed that it was a place for human burial only, and that pets, although also G-d's creatures and as such are also beloved, are not allowed to have that as their final resting place. But, eager to have his wishes come true, he tried another approach. "I'll give you a donation of $500." It was accepted, with an almost apologetic clarification, "oh, you didn't tell me the cat was Catholic."

* Entrepreneurs: I have developed two products that I will soon market. The first is a device to treat severe wounds that may be incurred while alone in the woods, far from medical facilities. It's called Suture Self. Another is a home treatment kit for those who cannot afford conventional orthodontics. It's called Brace Yourself.

*Admirers of Eastern religions: A Buddhist purchased a hot dog from a street vendor. When asked about condiments, he replied, "make me one with everything." And the mystic who asked that I treat him without using local anesthesia, for he "wanted to transcend dental medication."

* History Teachers: The entire story of Columbus has never been taught. Everybody knows about the three ships, the Nina, the Pinta and the Santa Maria, that made it to the new world, but there

were actually five vessels involved in the venture. Two had set sail a day before the famous three left, but before Columbus had discovered that the world was round, they fell off the edge.

* Physicians: "I have a great doctor. He had me on my feet in no time. I had to sell my car to pay his bill." "He became an anesthesiologist because he had trouble with anatomy and physiology in medical school, but he easily passed gas." "The only medical practitioner who should marry one of his patients is the gynecologist. At least he knows what he's getting into." "Anybody who goes to a psychiatrist should have his head examined." And, quoting Henny Youngman: "My doctor is a kind man. He told me I had six months to live. When I told him I could not pay my bill, he gave me another six months." "If you cannot afford the operation he will touch-up your x-rays."

* Investors: the story of George Washington throwing a silver dollar across the Potomac River is an oft-repeated legend. Modern day attempts to duplicate the feat have always been unsuccessful, and I believe the reason for the failure is the simple fact that money went further in those earlier days.

* Farmers: Max and Sam were lifelong friends. One day Max said that since they were getting on in years it would be a good idea to make a pact, that whichever one passed away first would try somehow to communicate with the living one, from wherever in the Great Beyond he should be. Sam agreed, and they never discussed it again. A while later Sam died. Max grieved for his friend and hoped that someday he may somehow be able

to hear from him. One evening, while sitting in his rocking chair, a faint voice was heard saying, "Max, Max." "Is that you Sam?" "Yes Maxie it's really me." "How are you doing Sam? Is everything okay?" "I'm doing great Max. I get up in the morning, have a large meal with plenty to drink. Then I go out into the field to play, and have sex all day long. When I return I have a big meal again, with even more to drink. This goes on every day." "Wow," said Max, "so that's what heaven is like?" "Heaven, what heaven?" came the reply, "I'm a bull in Montana."

* Blondes (very carefully): A man gave his blonde wife a cell phone, and provided her with instructions on its use. Later that afternoon, as she was leaving for shopping, he said that he would call her during the day just to see how her new device was working. As she wandered up and down the aisles with her shopping cart already filling up, her phone rang. Reaching into her bag, she removed the phone and answered it without a problem. With wonder in her voice, she told her husband how delighted she was with her phone, she would feel safe knowing that she had it, and that she would be home in about an hour. As she replaced it into her purse she stopped, pondered a moment, and seemed to be a bit puzzled. "Wait a minute. How did he know that I was in Walmart?"

* Grammar police: a patient was suffering from a spell of anxiety, and was instructed by his therapist to drink a cup of decaffeinated tea after a hot bath. When he returned for an evaluation a few weeks later, he was asked if he had followed the prescription. "I tried every day, without success.

Never got to the tea...could not finish drinking the bath."

* Beauticians: Mabel the hairdresser asked Sadie how she was able to keep her skin so smooth and wrinkle-free at her advanced age. "I take a milk bath once a week," she said. "Pasteurized?," Mabel asked. "No, just up to my chin."

* Horse Racing Fans: I have no luck at the racetrack. Once I bet on a horse that ran so slow that the jockey kept a log of the trip. Another time I bet on a horse that was so bad that he started in the third race and won the fourth. I also once bet on a horse that ran so late that when he came in he had to tip-toe into the stable.

* Gerontologists: a traveling salesman stopped overnight in a small town. Having time on his hands in the morning, he took his golf clubs and headed for the local course. Upon paying his fee he asked for a caddy, saying that he was a serious golfer and wanted the best one available. When he was introduced to his caddy, a slender, short, elderly gentleman who appeared to be close to 90 years old he became a bit dismayed. He turned to the golf pro and said that he felt that he was joshing him because he was an out of towner. "Oh, no," came the reply, "he's our best. He has the sharpest eyes of anyone on my staff. Go out on the course and enjoy." So the two of them went to the first hole. The salesman teed of and grunted as he sent the ball slicing into the woods. "Did you see where it went?" he asked. "Yup," came the reply. So they trudged to the area where the ball was last seen

heading. "Okay, so you saw where it went?" "Yup, I sure did." "Well, where is it?" "I forgot."

* Teachers' Aides: employment security is dependent on the annual school budget. To insure sticking with the job I suggest to ask for a transfer to the music department and become a band-aid.

* Attorneys (carefully, for my son Seth is a member of that esteemed profession): a brash elderly gentleman was standing before the bench and casting a few insults about the judge. When told by the magistrate that he had better be careful, for he could be held in contempt of court and fined or even jailed if he continued. "You mean I could be in trouble if I say bad things about you?" he asked. "That's right." "What if I just think bad things about you?" "Well I can't fine you if you just think bad things," said the judge. "Well then, I just think you're stupid."

What do a lawyer and a sperm have in common? One in two million have a chance to become a human being.

91% of lawyers give the rest a bad name.

(This category could go on and on.)

* College Faculty Members: it is a little known fact that the fraternity system was established at the very first university in our country. John Harvard realized that friendly competition among underclassmen was invigorating, and also helped promote social growth and maturity. With this in mind, he established the first two "Greek houses" on his campus: Tappa Kegga Beer and I Felta Thigh.

And finally, I must relate one quasi-joke that was sometimes heard in my office, and is, on close examination, not very humorous: What do you call the medical or dental student who graduated at the very bottom of his class? "Doctor."

During the last eighteen years of practice I was fortunate to have Barbara Weaver as my chair-side assistant. She is a very upbeat person, always finding something to be happy about. At first she was a bit reserved (professional?) but she soon realized that we could be light-hearted and still promote a feeling of trust and competency from our patients. For a while we were told that our approach reminded many of the television sit-com M.A.S.H. with its atmosphere of intensive surgery, heartfelt concern for patients, all blended with tension-relieving light-heartedness. She would keep a serious face if I were to respond to a patient's query with an answer that could be either funny or appear to be a bit demeaning, although the latter was never my modus operandi. When once asked by a patient if I had learned to be a dentist in the Army, I responded, "yes. I was a drill sergeant." There was no reaction, so I assumed my answer was informative. Another example occurred the day we were restoring a front tooth, using a light-sensitive material which had to be sculpted into place before being exposed to a curing light for completion. I often turned the dental lamp away so that polymerization of the filling would not begin prematurely. Since there was still enough ambient light for me to see, this could be done safely. As I moved the dental light away from the operative area, my patient became visibly concerned. "What are you doing? Why are you turning the light away?" I could not resist: "I had to. I learned how to do this procedure in night school." No reaction.

Since the weather was always an easy topic of conversation, many patients used it as an item for discussion as they were being seated. I developed a response to the ever-present complaint and everybody's observation whenever there was a snowstorm, heat wave, torrential rain or a cold snap: "Well, you can't change Mother Nature, it's too unpredictable," to which I always responded (sometimes with trepidation), "of course. However if the weather was logical it would be called Father Nature." This drew scorn from half of my patients, and laughter from the other half.

One of my favorite patients was Father Michael of St. Andrew Church, which was located just across the street from my office. He had a fine sense of humor, and always felt relaxed in my chair. My relationship with him was casual, informal, but always deferential. And how he loved to laugh! One time his secretary informed me that he was having a bit of pain from a tooth that was undergoing root canal therapy. My work day was finished, so I walked over to the rectory to deliver a packet of pain-relievers, and also to check in on him. I knocked on the door, and as he opened it he had a look of surprise on his face. Assuming a clerical posture, I handed him the medication and announced in a low voice that "the Lord had called to me and told me that there was a priest in pain. I was instructed to go forth and help." He laughed for what seemed like a full minute.

Dental bleaching was becoming an accepted dental modality, and was a frequent topic of conversation. So one day we realized that my priest friend was a good candidate for whitening. There were two methods in use, daytime and nighttime, each with a separate protocol. My presentation and instructions to Father Michael may have been a bit unclear, for I realized that I was confusing him. So I suggested the daytime method, and tailored an easy technique for him, which I linked to his Mass schedule: "Load the bleaching tray with the material and insert it into your mouth before you begin the processional. Remove the tray a few moments before you begin your homily and leave it out. As the service concludes, just before you stand up for the recessional, load and insert the bleaching tray again for another twenty minutes." After many years of service in Colchester he was transferred to another parish in another county. Before he left he presented me with a gift, a book entitled "Jewish Humor", which he autographed with the following inscription: To my friend Bernie. You need new material.

In my fifty-five years of dental practice there were many times when a patient's comment, joke or response to our banter was so clever that it had me laughing very hard. And if the retort was noteworthy I would say to the patient in a good-natured way, "don't get ahead of me pal. We're playing in my ballpark, and I own the baseball and the bat." But there was one moment that left me speechless, which my friends and family would find remarkable, if not unbelievable. Her name was Sally, a very intelligent, well-educated, refined wife of an attorney in nearby Norwich. She had been a most delightful patient for over forty years, and quite often joined in the conversation, whether it was humorous or intellectual or involved current events. In my later years of practice I had developed a routine that I used when replacing an older, non-serviceable restoration. I would often look at the patient's record to check the date of original treatment. It always gave me great pleasure to note that the work had lasted forty or thirty or twenty years, or whatever great number of years had passed. And if it was more than four decades old, I would state in jest that the work was done long ago, when we were all still youngsters. It somehow helped to soften the passage of time. So as Sally was relaxing with the nitrous oxide mask on her face, waiting for the local anesthetic to become effective, I began to spin my anecdote relating to the longevity of the now defective restoration. "You got your money's worth. Did this one forty-two years ago. I was ten and you were eight." Instead of the usual quiet smile which that always brought on, Sally just glanced at me and mumbled, "you damn fool." Her quick response startled me. "What do you mean?" I was quite taken aback, unable to interpret her remark. She looked at me and uttered what was undoubtedly the funniest statement I had ever heard in all my years of practice. "You were ten and I was eight. Right? You were playing dentist while all your friends were playing doctor." Priceless!

That contrasted with a remark that caught me off guard and also left me speechless, not for its lack of humor but for its stinging sarcasm. My hygienist Sheryl had signaled me to come into her room to examine a patient on whom she had just completed a dental prophylaxis. I looked at the name on the day's schedule, and as I walked to her operatory I prepared myself for a few minutes of unpleasantness. I knew that I would hear a litany of complaints from 'Mrs. Grouch'. The patient was a very wealthy older woman who begrudged having to part with any money. She once complained about the tax bill she had received from her town when she had sold forty acres of land. The transaction resulted in quite a profit, actually tripling her investment, but "oh the high taxes!" And dental fees were always much too high and just plain unreasonable, of course. So, trying to act pleasant, I began to initiate some small talk. After saying a warm hello, which I was able to force as I put on my mask and gloves. I could sense a slight undercurrent of tension. I tried to lighten the moment up a bit, so I asked her if she thought I would be able to go to the bank which was next-door, walk up to a teller, and with my face covered, demand a pile of money. She looked at me with an unpleasant stare and said, "why bother? Just go into the next room and rob another patient." That left me silent. Her attitude always reminded me of the joke about the woman who asked the waiter in a new seafood restaurant if they serve crabs. "We serve everyone ma'am, just have a seat."

Many patients also became friends. One such person was a sophisticated, fashionable woman named Barbara, who for more than a decade had been secretary to my lawyer and confidant Mel Scott. Thus a kinship had long ago been established, and we had all shared many laughs together at various social and political gatherings. I had gone through a period of depression during my mid-life crisis and one consequence was that I had put on a bit of weight, about forty pounds! Mel and Barbara were concerned, quite a bit more than I should have been, so much that, in addition to discussing the topic in a gentle, caring way, they purchased some dietary materials to help me return to a healthier life-style. Included was a video cassette program which had been developed by Suzanne Somers. Taking their advice, I began to focus on my problem, adding an exercise regimen to the daily viewing of the recorded instructions. After a few weeks I noticed that my clothes were fitting a lot better. Since I had been afraid to step on a scale because I felt that I might depress or sadden myself further, I used clothing comfort as a guide to my progress. One morning I noticed that there was no tightness. My outfit was very comfortable. So I rushed to the phone to call Barbara and tell her the good news. I said that I was very pleased, and that with a discernable shrinking waistline, "my pants seem to be getting looser." Her response was immediate: "I'm happy to hear that. When your pants become so loose that they fall down, give me a call." The three of us often recalled that line. Very funny, although very innocent.

Dentistry requires one to have compassion for the person sitting in the dental chair, and there was one fine example of the two-way flow of geniality. My patient was a middle-aged woman, tall in stature but short of courage, who, for twenty years, tolerated treatment with her hands tightly clenched and her mouth closed at every moment of opportunity. At times she would tense up so that her body went through a series of mini-shakes. But she was always compliant, and never refused or balked at any recommended treatment, albeit not without moaning and grumbling a bit. One day, as she was leaving, she turned to me and said in a quiet voice, "you're a very nice person, but you sure chose a lousy way to earn a living!" I laughed as she left without even a hint of a smile.

On several occasions I had to stifle a laugh in order not to embarrass a patient. One day a middle-aged woman with apparent challenged verbal skills presented for a consultation. Her complaint was that she had developed "sore gums." When I completed my exam I told her that periodontal surgery was indicated. I tried to explain in simple terms that part of the treatment would involve the removal of some gum tissue in order to correct the defect and also to allow her to practice good oral hygiene at home. When I asked if she had ever sought care for a similar problem in the past, she informed me that "a few years ago I was told that my gums were very bad, so I had a gingarectumy." The possibility that her former dentist had been working on the wrong end of the digestive system almost caused me to bite my tongue.

An interesting mental picture appeared when a man was discussing his fervor for the University of Connecticut's soccer, basketball and football programs. In addition to purchasing season tickets, he was also a contributor to the University's frequent fund raisers. He proclaimed that he was proud to be a "huge athletic supporter." Stifling a chuckle, I complimented him on his loyalty and enthusiasm. His cup runneth over.

Dental emergencies are never funny, but during my many years I can recall several that, although devoid of humor at the moment, later conjure up images that any afficionado of visual slapstick could enjoy. One warm summer day my secretary notified me that a local camp counselor had just come into the office with an eight year old boy who had just been injured playing baseball. The boy's mouth was bleeding. The lad was taken to the next room, where I tended to his immediate needs, a lacerated lip and two cracked front teeth. When all was finished, I inquired about the exact nature of the accident. The youngster was racing to catch a fly ball, arms held high in front of him, face looking skyward, when he ran right into a tree. But all ended well.

Another time a mechanic at a local gas station was brought in by a co-worker. The man had been in the process of removing a muffler from a car that had been placed on a lift, and had used so much force that when the part came loose it smacked him in the face, removing three of his teeth. In describing the incident the Samaritan reproduced the action in pantomime, while his friend, with his handkerchief held over his mouth gave him an angry, glaring look. But the strangest emergency call we ever received was from a person who announced that there was a patient on his way to the office with an emergency: he had just been hit by a house. The caller was a secretary in a local company that builds and sells sheds, garages and gazebos. The accident occurred when the worker was loading a small building onto a flat-bed truck for delivery. Somehow the weight shifted, and being close to the structure, he sustained his injury when the corner of the edifice slid against his face, causing his mouth to bleed. I gave the secretary an A plus rating for reporting accuracy, embellished as it might have been.

My relationship with patients was made more comfortable when I could connect with them in areas of common interests, especially sports, gardening, old movies, and travel, which would thus allow us to digress for a few relaxing moments before treatment. Since Colchester has a very large Polish population I had both a desire and an opportunity to learn enough words and phrases to be semi- conversational. Patients appreciated my attempt to become a kinsman of sorts, but one time I was caught in a situation which brought laughter to the patient as well as myself. In the chair was an older woman who was new to the practice. Her long last name, ending in 'ski', plus her Slavic features and slight accent beckoned me to greet her with the traditional Polish words, "yak shemash," how are you? There was no response. She looked at me with a blank stare, so I repeated "yakshemash pani,"adding the word for lady. Again there was silence. "Aren't you Polish?" I asked. Her response was immediate, unexpected and quite descriptive: "No, but my husband is. I'm Polish by injection." I stared at her smiling, blue-eyed, lightly lipsticked face, with its frame of softly combed white hair, and was frozen for at least ten seconds. From that moment on I spoke to her only in English.

Although the locale may change, dental humor is still possible. I was once "interviewed" by a prospective patient. It was in a social setting, about thirty minutes into the cocktail hour, when an attractive early middle aged woman walked over and introduced herself, saying that she wanted to leave her current dentist and have her records transferred to us, but before she could confirm the change she had to interview me. This was her standard procedure before engaging an attorney, a physician, or any other professional person. I told her that it was fine with me, and would do my best to pass any screening situation. "Great. Here's my question. What would you do if I were sitting in your chair and suddenly began gasping for breath and started screaming that I was in great pain and felt that I was about to die?" My response was immediate and concise: "If that were happening I would tell you that if you behaved I would take my foot off your throat." She was a patient for many years.

Again, another whimsical moment in a different environment. I was presented with an award of a kind which I never expected and in a place that I would have never envisioned. The location was a Board of Directors' meeting at Eastern Savings Bank in Norwich Connecticut. As a newly-appointed member, I had the added pleasure of serving with Linda Adelman, a retired nurse and now successful businesswoman, who had been a most delightful patient for over forty years. At the beginning of the session Linda stated that she wanted to make a presentation. She announced to the group that she was always both cognizant of and very pleased with the fact that my office kept up to date with modern technology. In addition, she always felt comfortable in knowing that I had earned a Fellowship from the Academy of General Dentistry and continued to learn and apply modern treatment modalities. She handed me the package, saying that "my gift to you is something to help you advance even more in your field." I placed the gift on the long table, to share the moment with the board. As I began to remove the wrapping paper, I broke out into laughter. I was now the owner of a brand new Hasbro Play-Doh Dr. Drill 'n Fill Kit. I assured Linda that it would somehow be used at her next dental appointment.

I had a built-in critic in my younger partner, Mike Babinski, who would often evaluate my material and offer a comment on its quality and merit. Mike, twenty years younger, was a big guy with an innocent altar-boy face and with an eclectic sense of humor. He was also my gyroscope, helping me keep on an even keel. He laughed, smirked, groaned, or just turned away in response to my latest witticism. And he performed this task for three decades. If I was in the process of repeating something I had related in the past, Mike would interrupt by shouting out, "number seven." This was a reference to his favorite tale of a comedians' convention where the attendees would take the stage, and since they all knew (and on occasion stole) each others' material, they would only have to bellow out the number of the joke instead of telling it. The first guest looked at the audience and announced, "number seventeen." The audience roared. The next person said, "number thirty four." Again a crescendo of laughter. "Number twenty seven" was the next offering. No response from the group. "Number twenty seven," the comic repeated. Again nothing. After he left the stage and sat down the next performer belted out, "number twenty seven," and almost immediately gales of laughter came from the crowd. "I guess some people can tell a joke, and some can't."

Mike had an annual Christmas joke, the telling of which marked the official start of the holiday season for me. But before I can relate it, I must first present a mini-tutorial in dental terminology. The surface of each tooth is designated by its relationship to the midline of the face: mesial is closer, distal is further, and by its relationship to the tongue (lingual) and cheek (buccal). The top surface is called the occlusal. In a system of shorthand, letters are used to record the surfaces on the dental record. MO is mesio-occlusal, etc. Mike's Yuletide harbinger: "What is a dentist's favorite Christmas carol? The first OL." (This was a bit of a technical exercise, but Mike's contribution to holiday hilarity deserves to be recorded for posterity). In Washington, DC, the lighting of the Christmas tree marks the beginning of the season. In Colchester, Connecticut it's the reference to "the first OL." My late wife Joan often noted that Mike was the brightest one, for he had a gift for being rational and unemotional when the situation required careful analysis and was thorough in his detailed explanation. Mike's humility was easy to put to the test, and when I would relate her statement to him he often responded by carefully evaluating her judgment: "I don't know.... she married you."

My first partner, Marty Zase, demonstrated early in our relationship that he had a sense of humor that would allow him to understand my verbal shenanigans, tolerate them, and also on occasion, expand upon them (listed in order of importance). As the practice grew I realized that bringing in an associate would not only help to handle a fast-growing patient load, but, and much more important, would provide me with a colleague with whom I could discuss any phase of dentistry at any time. This would also be a wonderful way of making continuing education programs even more of a meaningful learning experience. There would be someone with whom I could share and discuss new concepts and techniques, as well as lending a hand in planning or assisting in difficult clinical procedures. What a luxury to have intra-office consultations.

So one morning he asked me to take a look at a patient for whom he was developing a treatment plan, and who presented a bit of a puzzle. There were notches in the enamel of the person's two upper front teeth. Were they developmental or the result of extrinsic physical stresses? Should they be crowned or simply restored? After examining the situation I took Marty aside and said that I believed they were notches caused by outside forces, and I felt that two crowns in non-traumatic occlusion was the indicated treatment. I went on to tell him that I was certain of my diagnosis because I had a clinical instructor at Penn, a Venezuelan graduate student, who taught me the classification of enamel defects. "His name was Dr. Buay. He was an expert...in fact we used to say that 'Buay knows notches'." The next morning I received a telegram. The sender was a man named Dr. Buay. The message was brief: "Thank you for remembering me after all these years." I immediately realized that there were now two pranksters in the office.

As the decades began to flit by, I found that adapting to the latest trends in music, fashion, and even practice settings was necessary, and although a bit resistant to the growing informality that was wending its way across our country, I soon began to enjoy the shift away from the white-starched clinical attire of my previous academic and professional environment. Early in my practice I took a leap forward by allowing my dental assistants, at their request, to wear slacks and colorful scrub tops. I wore bell-bottom pants, owned three leisure suits, grew sideburns, and learned to enjoy as well as play and even dance to the contemporary music that patients wanted to hear, the tempo and lyrics of which were so far removed from my favorite tunes of the 40's and 50's that I had thought would never be displaced.

I realized that I was now part of the new world when one of my patients who had just returned from Vietnam presented me with a welcome-back present: an envelope containing six marijuana cigarettes. It was something that I had tried a few times before, and although I recalled the pleasant feeling that it brought on, it was not for me. Besides the possibility of addiction, I concluded that it was difficult to regulate and evaluate the effect due to the method of usage. I fared much better with a glass of fine bourbon, three ice cubes, and a splash of what Lyndon Johnson called branch water. That is an easy mixture to titrate! However, not wanting to dispose of my gift (just in case I changed my mind), I hid them. For many years my partners delighted in describing my method: I filed them away in a cabinet and in a folder marked "J", which I told them stood for "joint."

A professional person in a small town invariably becomes involved in several civic activities. As a Justice of the Peace, the state of Connecticut had granted me the privilege of performing wedding ceremonies. Often this provided me with the opportunity to veer off on a playful tangent. One male patient complained that his wife often referred to their wedding vows as permission to pile many household chores upon him daily. "The wording should be changed from 'I do' to 'I will have to'." I told him that I had written a more practical set of instructions for the groom: "You have the right to remain silent. Anything you say or even think will be held against you."

On one occasion the joke du jour almost backfired. My patient was a young man who had been courting his sweetheart for about two years, and was now beginning to be pressured into setting a date. He loved her and knew that he would someday marry her, but he was not yet ready to settle down. I told him about one of my favorite Abbott and Costello skits that had been on television a few decades before, where Lou Costello compared marriage to a three ring circus: "There's the engagement ring, the wedding ring, and suffering." He enjoyed this so much that he used it to buffer his procrastination. His partner-to-be was also a patient in my office, and informed me that this time I was not funny. But all ended well, for they were married two years later. They told me that the three ring circus quote had been heard so often that they had it written into their ceremony. And they lived happily ever after.

When discussing marriage ceremonies I would sometimes reveal to my newly-betrothed Jewish patients that I had completed research into the significance of the dramatic moment at the end of the ceremony, when the groom smashes a glass with his heel just before kissing his bride The two traditional and still prevailing theories are that the event commemorates the destruction of the Temple of Jerusalem, or that it is a wish that the couple's happy moments may be as numerous as the shards of glass. Not so. My studies show that it depicts the last time the groom will have a chance to put his foot down. (Why am I not laughing?)

Politics is an attraction for many small-town professionals. Name recognition, a huge factor in elections, is not an issue. And the opportunity to become involved in helping make another human being's little slice of the world a better place is exciting. As Chairperson of the Colchester Board of Education I had another platform (pun intended) from which I could begin to play a larger role. It had always been a sad perception for me when I encountered so many people through the years who had regretted inaction of some sort in an earlier stage of their life. "I wish I had, etc." always left me with a tinge of sadness for the individual. In 1958 I read Edwin O'Connor's novel "The Last Hurrah" which was inspired by the life of Boston's late mayor James Michael Curley, a rogue who lived a tumultuous political life, but was always seeking to help "the little people." Having grown up in Boston during those years I was fascinated by his larger-than-life approach to challenges. In the novel, as he lay dying, eyes closed and about to breathe his last, the Cardinal who had administered last rites leaned over him and stated in a whisper that "if he had to live his life all over again there's no doubt in the world he would do it very, very differently." The mayor opened his eyes, and with a bit of a smile said, "like hell I would." Then his eyes closed, and he passed on with a hint of the smile still on his lips. This no doubt became a subliminal mantra for me, for in 1986, while still the senior partner in a very busy three-doctor practice, I ran for the Connecticut Legislature!   I was fulfilling a dream.

A few weeks before the primary election, as a candidate for the state legislature, I was a VIP guest at a Democratic party rally that was held at the firehouse in Salem, one of the three towns in the House district. As expected, the hall was full of the beautiful people plus the legions of wannabes. Among those present were Governor Bill O"Neill, Senator Chris Dodd, Congressman Sam Gejdenson, several state representatives and state senators, plus a cadre of town selectmen, town clerks, and assorted other local officials, registrars of voters, tax collectors and justices of the peace. Filling in the crowd were many dozens of citizens and the ever-present political junkies who like to wear political pins on their caps and shirts and make small-talk with the movers and shakers. Local television stations were on hand to record a few minutes of local history. As the time came for the speeches, we were treated to a predictable stream of energizing political rhetoric, defining our mission and expounding upon how the people in that building would make this a better planet. Been there, heard that. Then it was the moment for the candidates for various state offices to speak. After listening to the passion with which Senator Dodd delivered his remarks, and he was a dynamic speaker, I decided to take a quieter approach, hoping that the contrast would make my remarks more listenable. As I stood on the stage looking around at the array of dignitaries, I told the crowd that I was very, very proud of all our elected Democratic officials, national, statewide, and local, but that there was one whom I considered to be a political giant---Governor William O"Neill. "I have the highest respect and admiration for any man who has the power to take away my license to practice dentistry in the state of Connecticut." That statement generated a robust wave of applause and cheers. I felt like a real politician. But that was the highlight of my legislative venture. A month later I lost the election by a few hundred votes. But I ran for a high office, and have no regrets. I will never say "I wish I had...."

A few years later I was a guest at a district-wide a retirement party for Governor O"Neill. All the Democratic Town Committee chairpersons were asked to bring a gift or two that was representative (pun intended) of their city or town. And so I brought a dozen eggs from a Colchester farm, plus a pumpernickel bread from the renowned Colchester bakery. But I could not resist an opportunity to add some humor to the event. I had a third gift for the Governor. As I presented it I told the gathering that for many years the Governor had always been gracious when asked to pose for photographs of himself with many individuals. So many would hang them on their office or home walls as a sign of their importance. To commemorate this kind gesture, and with gratitude, I then handed him a picture of myself which I had signed, "to my good friend Bill from Bernie Park." His Irish eyes twinkled and he gave me a hug. Political career over, now back to my office.

I have been blessed with an excellent memory, though now and then it may seem to be a curse. As the years passed by some patients would change their hairstyles or alter the tint, or would either by exercising or by wearing more stylish apparel, be able to improve their physical image. This invariably caught my attention and I would take the opportunity to compliment them in a most heartfelt manner. The usual reaction was one of appreciation, for although I may not have seen the person for six months or more, not only had I remembered how they had appeared in the past, I now also commented on the pleasant change and I always commended them. Once in a while a few patients would remark, with just a hint of shyness that I was just saying that to flatter them. My standard response would serve to underline my sincerity: "Since I'm not involved in politics any more, I now have the luxury of always being able to tell the truth." The patient's quick smile registered a vote of approval. (Pun intended.)

Dentistry was fulfilling in so many ways. I enjoyed taking continuing education courses throughout the years, and went on to earn a fellowship in the Academy of General Dentistry. I remembered very well the admonition given to us at Penn by the dean, Dr. Lester Burket, that "a professional person has no right to be other than a continual student." The every-day relationships with my patients and my staff provided an ongoing source of energy, and I treasured their friendship and trust. Keeping abreast of the exploding technological advances through five decades of practice was always energizing, so much that in my later years I often told patients that my profession had advanced so dramatically that the only thing I still used in my work today that I had used when I was in dental school was my name. I also learned that in daily practice one is limited only by his imagination. I thought so often of Einstein's belief that imagination was more important than knowledge. It has no limits. "Logic will get you from A to B; imagination will take you everywhere."

However, there were times when I believed it was best not to let people know how I earned a living. This was a reaction to a few awkward situations when I realized that it was better for my psyche to adopt an innocuous attitude. For many years I relished the opportunity to announce to anyone within earshot that my name was Doctor Park, and that I was a dentist, on ski trips or camping vacations or even sitting at Fenway Park watching a Red Sox game. Eventually I discovered that this too often led to a wave of questions from strangers, such as, "why does a root canal cost so much?" or, "why does my insurance not cover 100% of my dentist's charges?" or, "why do I need a crown instead of a filling?" Reasonable queries, but it was not easy to respond, for I had no idea what they had been told in the past. And then there were the less-than-reasonable (disrespectfully referred to as dumb) ones: "Why does it cost so much to fix baby teeth?" "Why does my dentist charge so much?" "How much do you charge for a filling?" And my all-time favorite:"Do you fix your own teeth?"

There was one difficult moment when I realized that I had made a mistake by revealing my profession. It made me a victim of deflected anger. The 13th century Persian poet and theologian

Rumi had written that "you are not a drop in the ocean. You are the ocean in a drop." The meaning of his words came to me in a strange way, and in a strange place. It took place on a bus tour traveling from Venice to Florence in Italy. I had been seated behind an older gentleman from New York who seemed to be pleasant, and tried to engage anyone nearby in random conversation. Having stated with a bit of pride that I was a dentist from Connecticut, I was not prepared for the tirade that ensued. He turned around to me and in an angry tone of voice announced that all dentists were crooks, that he had been overcharged by his dentist back home who made him a partial denture that did not fit. Then, to my continued chagrin, he removed the appliance from his mouth to show it to me, and stated that it was a piece of junk. He wanted to know why this happened. It took a few minutes before I was able to convince him that I was on vacation, and my privacy was being violated. It was then that I postulated a Bernie Park theorem: "Never miss a chance to keep your mouth shut."

Years later I followed my own advice. I found myself in a situation when I knew that revealing my vocation would lead to conversation that I would find to be uncomfortable, unwanted and unrewarding. The setting was the Waldorf Astoria hotel in New York City. The situation was a lavish wedding reception for a cousin-in-law. It was an event that I would rather have evaded and was seated with people whom I would have avoided, if either had been possible. As the meal was being served I had to listen to what I soon considered to be boring conversation, one person trying to outdo the others with tales of business accomplishments and financial success. One had just opened his third beauty salon, and another had purchased a brand new Cadillac, .etc. As I sat quietly, I realized that they would eventually want to hear about my achievements in life. And sure enough, the moment arrived. "And what do you do for a living?" I was determined to put some verbal distance between myself and the inquisitive entrepreneurs. "I cannot discuss what I do," was my response. Their looks revealed their heightened curiosity. "But we told you all about us." Somehow a few gears in my head turned and produced a reply. "But I didn't ask you. However, not to be rude, I will answer your question, but you must not ask me anything more about my job." Now their glances turned to full-attention stares. Straightening up in my chair, I took a sip of bourbon, and in a measured voice stated, "I'm with the C I A." I found the remainder of the afternoon to be rather enjoyable. It was then that I resolved that I would discuss dentistry either at courses or meetings with my colleagues, for whom I have high regard, or in my office with my patients, for whom I have great appreciation.

Patient participation in the chatter that Barbara and I kept up as a form of mini-distraction always blended in with the appointment, and the themes were as varied as the moment dictated. We would often create a thread, inviting patient participation. For example, there was the mythical person who's life was computer driven: his wife was named Meg. She was a waitress, so she worked as a server, who had undergone a breast reduction procedure to correct her floppies. His chauffeur was in charge of the drivers, and he went to his dentist often to check the byte, and to his chiropractor to check his discs. He would relax by playing in a rock band, always performing the same old gig.

We would create a dialogue that was often repeated to relax and distract the patient as we three waited for the local anesthetic to become effective. This would serve to speed up the passing of the few minutes required before we could begin our work, and help to soften any possible anxiety that was often a normal response to the impending experience. One of our favorites was our "research into heretofore untold Biblical events and interpretations," which was presented as one long homily. In the beginning the was nothing, and darkness was on the face of the earth. And then G-d created light, and there was still nothing, but now you could see it. And the first incidence of jealousy occurred in the Garden of Eden, when Eve said to Adam, "what do you mean the boys do not look like you?" And then there was Moses, the greatest magician in the Bible. It was reported that Moses crossed the desert, came to an oasis, tied his ass to a tree, and then walked away. And of course Samson, the first great actor, who brought down the house. Even the account of Noah had to be clarified. It is written that all the animals came into the ark in pairs. Not quite true, for the worms came in apples. And the commandment to go forth and multiply caused some distress for the snakes who lamented that they could not obey because they were adders. And the early Jews fought among themselves. David slew Goliath, one of the Finkelsteins.

One unique thread lasted a few years because some patients participated to the extent that they would add to the list every six months, increasing its length as they invented a new submission which they brought with them to their check-up visits. I'm referring to the mythical humorous description of the termination of a worker's career. For example, the electrician who retired was delighted. The lawyer was debriefed. I will list a few of the most representative:

The spy was debugged
The camp counselor was debunked.
The musician was decomposed.
The shoe salesman was defeated.
The cosmetologist was defaced.
The judge was defined.
The nuclear plant worker was degenerated.
The teacher was degraded.
The exotic dancer was denuded.
The wine salesman was deported.
The appliance repair man was deranged.
The politician was devoted.
The gambler was discarded.
The hair stylist was distressed.
The credit manager was discharged.
The tour guide was dislocated.
The fisherman as debated.
The exam proctor was detested.
The dressmaker was depleated.

And one more, a bit different, which will be revealed later, when I report a few of the exchanges that occurred over several decades of pun-a-thons with my two greatest patient "wordversaries"—Bob and Mark.

There were routines which seem to have developed themselves over the years. One of our silliest (and therefore relaxing) would kick in whenever a conversation turned to a discussion involving the innocence and beauty of a new-born baby. I was not a pretty baby:

I was such an ugly baby that when I was born my mother was given a ticket for littering. I was such an ugly baby that when I was born the doctor slapped my mother.

I was such an ugly baby that they often diapered the wrong end.

I was such an ugly baby that once when my father said, "I think the baby needs changing," my mother informed him that they would not take me back.

I was such an ugly baby that my mother tried to have an abortion that same day.

And there was one that would always cause Barbara to laugh hysterically every time for many years: I was such an ugly baby that when the stork delivered me he flew with one wing covering his eyes. As I said the lines I covered my eyes with my elbow in a wing-like gesture. Barbara's laugh could be heard as far away as the front desk.

We had also created a companion lament: the unwanted child:

I knew I was unwanted when my parents gave me an electric train with 50 miles of straight track.

I was kidnapped. When my parents got the ransom note they sprung into action: they immediately rented out my room.

My allowance was given to me in travelers' checks.

My parents began searching for summer camps in December.

One day I got lost at the beach. I asked the policeman if he could help me find my parents. He replied, "I think so. There aren't too many places where they could hide."

Most of the repartee was generated spontaneously, and words and ideas often linked together quite easily. For example, mention of the word 'anatomy' lead to the following verbal quiz:

What part of the body is the fray? A news article said that the general was shot in the thick of the fray.

What part of the body is the fancy? In the movie the lover said that he tickled her fancy.

What part of the body is the now? The song asks, "I wonder who's kissing her now?"

And continuing in the same nonsensical spirit, that lent itself to the fabrication of a fictitious moment in political history, the concocted fact about Henry Kissinger's double. Many political leaders have body doubles that serve to throw off the media or potential trouble-makers when the real personage is traveling to other countries to conduct affairs of state. So one morning the former Secretary of State's three stand-ins checked the daily work schedule to see who was on duty that day. As one asked, "I wonder who's Kissinger now."

Occasionally the attempt to generate a chuckle by constructing a concept, and with an oblique twist, transform it into a witticism did not work. Either the reference was to a situation or expression that a young person might not understand, or it required some knowledge beyond the patient's academic prowess. As an example I have listed a few of my better (?) ones:

Brutus met Caesar after breakfast, and asked him how many eggs he had eaten. "Et tu Brute," he replied.

Why does a Frenchman eat only one egg? Because in French one egg is un oeuf.

My favorite Christmas carol is the one about the member of King Arthur's roundtable who had just gotten married. You know, Silent Knight.

Mark Antony was asking the Roman people to help him get some form of nitrogen to help fertilize his garden, when he said, "friends, Romans, countrymen, lend me urea."

Archeologists have discovered the first record of sports scores. It was a report of a contest in ancient Rome. Researchers unearthed a tablet near the Coliseum from the year 70 which read "Lions 14, Christians 0."

I can cite a few more allusions that went unrecognized. "I guess Will Rogers never met you." This was a veiled admonishment that I used when dealing with someone who was pestering me. The reference was to the late humorist, who in 1927 had said, "I never met a man that I didn't like." It was effective in my early practice years when the patient population was older than I and could easily identify and understand the implication. Another misunderstood statement resulted from my keeping a bottle of water nearby, both to keep myself hydrated in hot weather and also to suppress a cough that had been induced by seasonal allergies. Since water ranks lower on my pleasure scale than tea, coffee, or bourbon, once I brought the container to my lips I would drink as much as I could tolerate. If asked why I took so much at one time, I would quote Aristotle. "One swallow does not a summer make." Most of the time I would receive a puzzled look.

My advice was always to "go with the flow." If the subject du jour was a military action somewhere in the world I would remark that to me the most unusual cause of any conflict occurred in 1789: the French Revolution was brought on by a shortage of cake.

When the Wright Brothers staged their first flight in 1903 one entrepreneur wanted to start a coast to coast airline, but was stymied when he realized that it would be too difficult, having to land and take off every 852 feet. In writing these I realize now that some of them do take quite a bit of thinking.

And now the puns! This delightful (?) form of wit was an ever present part of my daily practice routine. Although some may claim this to be the lowest form of humor, I found it applicable because so many patients could often sense when one was coming. It gave me pleasure to watch, for a smile would crawl across their lips as they awaited the punch line. A few even groaned before I could complete my delivery. To elevate the pun to its proper status, I quote a literary giant whose writings were not often associated with humor, but who was respectful of the nature of the art, Edgar Allen Poe, who stated that "the goodness of the true pun is in the direct ratio of its intolerability." Through the years I kept a journal of what can be described as a melange of playful pronouncements. The stimulus for each gem is long forgotten, but they still can stand alone as mechanisms for injecting (pun intended) a relaxing beat or two into the pulse of a dental appointment. The order is as haphazard as the event that produced them.

Saw a dental soap opera on tv—The Edge of Bite.

I showed him the x-rays of hopeless teeth--previews of coming extractions.

A great Christmas present—Santa floss.

Music to rinse by—a spit tune.

If I accidentally dropped a few cotton pellets and the patient swallowed them, would I be tried in appellate court?

If I made a commercial advertising dentures made in one day, could I call it Fasteeth?

Dental x-rays made me think of a detective who had just solved a case, saying, "looks like an inside job."

Didn't want his wisdom teeth extracted, for he was attached to them.

A protein is a 17 year old who signs a major league contract.

Beyond redemption means the date on the discount coupon has gone by.

The dental anesthetic comes in small glass containers. That's why it has a vile taste.

My optometrist friend went camping, and provided care for patients in his tent. It was a site for sore eyes.

Imagine a clinic that specialized in full dentures and made its own dental adhesive. Patients could get goop rates. They could discuss the emotional stress of having loose plates in goop therapy, and if unhappy could try to regoop their money.

I hold the crown in place with my finger until the cement sets because this is the digital age.

Do you really floss, or are you just stringing me along?

Orthopedic surgeons do not operate alone: it is a joint effort.

And the nurse was part of the cast.

He felt that like a dentist because he dealt with so many knee caps.

Music playing in the background was Elvis singing "Love My Tendon."

And he had a tendoncy to sing while he was working.

The gynecologist had a gentle nature. He would never stirrup any trouble.

You could never find a placenta person.

The funny bone is given that name because it is next to the humerus.

There was a production of the musical Hair done on Broadway in the mid-twenties. It was called "Ziegfield's Follicles."

We arranged the mouth mirrors in the drawer properly, .in new-mirrorcal order.

Would not get into a discussion of the biblical account of the parting of the Red Sea. The subject is too deep.

Your remark that tooth-brushing should be done only once a day makes me bristle.

Teachers in a German barber school are called Herr Professor. To get a promotion they had to work their way up the lather.

The dental allusion to the United Kingdom's royal family...a succession of crowns. Could their history be referred to as a crown-ology? Was the royal physician an endocrownologist?

My friend was a gourmet cook, but his constant bragging was annoying. He made a pesto himself.

Analogy refers to inference, such as why does ragweed make you sneeze, .analogy?

My last (and best) chair-side assistant, Barbara Weaver, provided me with eighteen years of skillful clinical proficiency. She would in later years describe how her first impression of my approach to the practice of dentistry made her a bit uneasy: I was so "professional" in my selection and manner of asking questions and pursuing erudite informational exchanges that she revealed later that when she returned home she told her husband that this might not be an office that she would enjoy. "This guy is a dud." But by the second interview I felt that our temperaments would eventually blend, and that we could function quite nicely in our treatment regimen. Welcome to the office.

I felt that Barbara had a bit of a whimsical nature, and that I would soon get her to relax enough to just be herself. She had worked for a few dentists before, so there was a level of built-in practice attitudes that were a bit different from mine. However, we happened upon a wonderful opportunity to get to know each other better. A few weeks after her first day of work, we drove to Boston to attend a course at Tufts Dental School. This would give us many hours to talk, but, of greater importance, would present a wonderful opportunity to have a clinical discussion on the way back to Colchester. Perhaps feeling a bit nervous, Barbara brought a few Christmas gift catalogues to browse through as we rode, perhaps to fill in a few awkward moments of the trip. But she spent a lot of time browsing. I was not offended. It was a ninety minute ride.

When we got to the parking garage I drove to the upper floor, and than circled slowly, looking for the perfect parking spot, one with space on both sides, or even what I refer to as "an end cut."

This fascinated Barbara, and she joined in the hunt, pointing out possible landing sites. But I must admit I do have a hang-up when it comes to parking, especially in a crowded garage in a big city. Barbara was beginning to enjoy our search, and began making little cute comments. I could feel a sense of relaxation. We were both enjoying the whimsical chiding. As we walked to the elevator I admitted that I often make parking more difficult than it should be. She replied with a wise-crack. OK...game on. When the elevator doors opened we got in, along with about fifteen other people. I was quiet as we rode down, and than as the doors opened and the group began to exit slowly, I said in a not-too-quiet voice, "Barbara, we are in Boston. Your parole officer told me to remind you that if you stay out of trouble you will not have to go back to prison." Suddenly everybody began to move quickly away from Barbara, staring at her as they whisked by. Barbara's face turned red, then began to pale. She began to scrunch down a bit, trying to make herself a bit shorter. We walked together quietly, and then I asked her for an analysis of my parking skills once more. At that moment, we changed the stereotypical doctor/assistant scenario and established the professional/friendly relationship that lasted for so many years.

Thus, the stage was set for a practice environment that would help minimize patients' fears and feelings of isolation. And equally important, she became a partner in crime in helping to create those lighter moments for seemingly anxious patients. I often referred to her as "my right hand, who sits on my left," for she had the ability to shift from a formal mode to a whimsical posture as the situation would dictate. As an example, when I once extended my left hand to receive an instrument, she placed a quarter into it. That required a change of glove. Another time I held out my hand and she took it into hers and shook it. When I called out for an explorer (the dreaded "dental pick") she blurted out, "Christopher Columbus." We had a mini-routine that was comprised of my peering into a mouth, remaining quiet for a moment or two, after which Barbara and I would say in unison "looks like an inside job."

She would then look plaintively at the patient, saying, "he makes me say that." Another part of our routine (with the right patient) had me moving the mirror throughout the patients mouth, and then exclaiming, "oh no; oh my goodness." Barbara would then turn to me, and with a quizzical look on her face ask what was wrong. My reply was simple:"I forgot to mail an important letter this morning." The look on the patient's face would range from a smile to a scowl, and was usually accompanied by a shake of the head. (I did preface this by saying "with the right patient.")

Barbara had invented a few gags of her own. My routine always involved chatting as I put on my mask and gloves, all the while making eye contact with the person sitting in the dental chair. One morning, as I was placing the mask over my mouth, the patient and Barbara both began laughing hysterically. I could not begin to understand what was going on, but I soon caught on when I realized that they were both looking at my face. Barbara had used a black magic marker to paint kitty whiskers on the front of the mask, and then placed the mask face down on my counter. So the single motion of donning the mask while exchanging pleasantries created laughter that could be heard throughout the office.

However, her greatest piece of mischief involved my operating gloves. Although I had a dispenser on the wall within easy reach, Barbara often set up the mask and gloves on my counter in the morning before my first patient was seated. When the synergy of time and proper person lined up, she carried-off the best prank that anyone had ever played on me. I was facing the patient and talking (as always) as I began to put on the glove. When I snapped it on my middle finger popped out and presented a gesture that is universally recognized as obscene. Barbara had cut the glove, and as I placed my hand into it my own exposed middle finger rose into the air in a rather dramatic fashion A feeling of embarrassment immediately gripped me, but then I had to laugh. For the first time ever I knew what Stephen King meant when he wrote, "if you want to play, you gotta pay."

In a more relaxed fashion Barbara and I would create a thread of puns as we worked, yet never allowing ourselves to be distracted from the task of hand. Patients would often join in, and the fun came in trying to squeeze out one more witticism when the list began to appear full. I kept a record of one such exchange and present it only as an example of diversionary dialogue, and not an attempt to secure a spot in some hallowed hall of hilarity. The topic was fish:

I make these jokes just for the halibut.
They are the best one to come down the pike.
Stay on the subject, don't flounder around.
These are the bass ones.
We're coming up with a good grouper two.
And they're free. No perch is necessary.
Eel understand them.
Share them. Don't be shellfish.
You don't have to wait your turn. Just mussel in.
They're beginning to give me a haddock.
Holy mackerel, it got a ten on the joke scale.
I believe we may be finnish.
Like the background music? I chose salmon-chanted evening.
No? I should have played a different tuna.
I take sole responsibility.
Walleye guess we're done.
What's the porpoise of these puns?
If you find out, let minnow.

And then there is the list of schools where students could find specialized training for a particular field of interest. For example:

Asian food production...Rice
Highway construction...Tulane
Prison Administration...Penn State
Cheese manufacturing...Colby
Sports injuries...Sorbonne
Abrasives...Emory
Fishing Industry...Bates

Scandinavian Prisons...Yale
Mixology...Manhattanville
Tooth Brush Design...Tufts
German History...Oberlin
Baseball equipment...MIT
Chicken production...Purdue
Clergyman...Temple
Pre-veterinary studies...De Pauw
Clarinet players...Reed
Marriage Counselor....Union
Metal forging...Smith
Home management...Butler
Automobile sales...Haverford
And my favorite: home heating systems...Yeshiva

During five decades of practice the visits were made pleasant, and sometimes even memorable, when so many patients enjoyed joining in the lighthearted banter. But there were two individuals whose aptitude for spontaneous humor which coupled with quick responses (timing—the keystone of comedy) were so remarkable that my assistants would often have to close the operatory door after seating the patient. The roar of laughter could be heard across the hall. Their names are Bob LaMay and Mark Lander. Bob had been a patient for 30 years, and Mark held the record—-51 years! Not only was the room set up for the dental procedure, but I also kept a pencil and a pad of paper on the counter on my right, ready to take notes at any moment. With hope that someday I would write a book, I chronicled the more noteworthy (pun intended) exchanges. They were so fast and incisive that every session provided fresh material. To assure time for the development of all possible comic interchanges each visit, I always added fifteen minutes to that day's appointment. That was my personal form of dental insurance.

With an ever-present impish glint in his eyes and an animated way of speaking, Bob often caught me off-guard when responding to a routine inquiry. Once, after waiting the usual few minutes for the local anesthetic to become effective, I asked, "Are you numb?" Without a bit of hesitation he shot back, "I don't know. I can't feel anything." Or, after having completed a procedure, I always asked the standard question, "How does the bite feel?" He would then rub his finger along the tops and edges of his upper and lower teeth and report, "Feels okay." After the preparation of a tooth for a crown was completed, I told Bob that I had to select a shade in order to match the restoration to his other teeth. With a whimsical smile and a quick series of wisecracks he launched into a Grouch Marx type of banter: "Shave? I took a shave this morning. It was a hair-raising experience. I just stubbled along." At times I would just look at him, and, expecting to hear something funny I would just begin to laugh. When he asked me what was so humorous, I informed him that I had just told myself a joke. "And it was one that I had never heard before."

B ob was a railroad buff, and had even published a book on the history of locomotives. So it was not surprising that trains were often the vehicle (again, intended) for a moment ot two of distraction. Some of the proclamations were predictable: "My teeth feel great. You must be on the right track." Some were admirable stretches: "Elvis Presley sang about trains. Remember 'Love My Tender'?" "I made up these puns without any coaching." "I wish the puns could be much better, but diesel do." "In Mexico a man hijacked a train. His reason for doing so did not make any sense...might say it was a locomotive." "Making railroad puns is the ticket to relaxation. Gets rid of a lot of baggage." It was in this environment that I fabricated one of my worst puns. I told Bob that I had a friend who worked as a railroad engineer, and who had two children that were always pestering him to bring home gifts from his travels. He was annoyed with their constant requests but he still brought something home for them after every trip. There was never a Lackawanna. But I must say that he often outpaced me in our exchanges. His were more streamlined.

Mark taught French and English at Bacon Academy, Colchester's public high school. He was an excellent teacher, quite popular, who also functioned as track coach and advisor to the National Honor Society. Tall, and with perfect posture, he had a professional (stern?) appearance that belied his sense of humor. His manner of speaking was precise, measured and direct. One time, as I was completing a root canal, he smiled and in a soft voice said, "The thought of you working in a canal that you cannot see is Erie." At another visit I was polishing a restoration, a procedure that tends to splatter the paste over the tongue. He mused that, "I'm not hungry any more. I can taste the sandwich is in my mouth." He would tell me about the poet who, "woke up in the morning and went from bed to verse. But that's an ode story." At another visit he suggested that, "When preparing a crown you should wear Regal shoes. But when cementing it you have to slipper on." "But rather than lacing into his statement, eyelet that remark go."

Occasionally the puns took the form of a dialogue:

"The tailor was broke. He depleated his funds."

"That sounds like an off the cuff remark."

"I'm not trying to skirt the issue."

"Seams alright."

"Suit yourself."

"I have a vested interest in this story."

"He charges a low price. He should jacket up."

One day I found a way to embarrass him in his classroom, while at the same moment I was in my office working. Mark had joined in the thread which I had mentioned earlier, the list of former occupations, and how each practitioner had ended his career. At his last visit he came up with his own roster. It described the former teacher who was degraded, outclassed, unprincipalled, had lost his faculties, became detested, and as a result, had no class. Very nice. Now he was getting ahead of me. Later that afternoon the school courier brought some inter-office mail, a packet that I received often in my capacity as Board of Education Chairperson. If I had correspondence that required an immediate response, the courier would return a bit later and take it to the proper department. I took paper in hand and wrote down a few words, then addressed the letter to Mark Lander at Bacon Academy, and marked it urgent. I was told the next day that the dispatch had been placed on his desk during a classroom period. When he opened it and read the message, he began to choke with laughter, much to the amusement of his students. He could not reveal the reason for his response. I had sent one more occupation question. "What happened to the prostitute who retired? She was delayed."

On many visits either Mark or I would somehow establish a topic, and then some free-wheeling repartee would begin. I said, "Hawaii," and immediately I heard, "Aloha. Hawaii today? I would complain but Waikiki?" The word Egypt led to a story relating to Marc Antony and Cleopatra. He thought he did not love her, but he was in de Nile. One day they had quarreled, and she was lying down on a couch when he entered the room. He appeared angry, but she was able to soothe him, saying, "I'm not inclined to argue." That set the stage for me to describe the results of a study which I had just completed. I had undertaken some research in Egyptology, and directed my work toward interpreting hieroglyphics. After careful examination I concluded that the picture writing was all in capital letters. If there were any in lower case they would be called loweroglyphics.

It was in this setting that I concocted what I believe to be my most outrageous farcical rearrangement of historical and fabricated facts. Stretching my investigation back a few thousand years I discovered that it was the Egyptians who had invented the garage door opener. In ancient Egypt the chariots were an independent unit in the rulers' forces. This enabled them to travel considerable distances, do their plundering, and return home laden with the bounty of battle. However, there were instances when they had been overwhelmed, and had to race home at great speed, for they were being pursued. As they returned they dashed for the safety of the great pyramid, on the front of which was inscribed Tutenkhamen.

In my early years of life I discovered that I was a bibliophile long before I even knew the term existed. Reading was an important part of my young development, and as a result I had a penchant for the use of the proper word at the proper time. Also, I was extremely fortunate to have had excellent teachers in the Boston public school system, the old-fashioned kind that loved to teach and were dedicated to and proud of their profession. Somehow I developed a fascination for linguistic amalgamations (pun intended). A friend once described this as my having a funnel screwed in on top of my head. Words are poured in, mix together, and emerge in a humorous and creative form. Word association was automatic, and always in overdrive. As a result, when I took the Miller Analogies Test for graduate school many years later my score was high enough to qualify me for membership in Mensa. I write this only as prelude to my description of the most outlandish (different from outrageous) pun which I believe I have ever concocted, a combination of verbal and visual elements.

Mark was sitting in the dental chair, and in the background music the selection playing was a rendition of "It Might As Well Be Spring." Without prompting or warning,the funnel opened. I related to Mark the sad tale of a young man who wanted to buy a gift for his sweetheart, and thought that one of the new quartz watches that had just come onto the market would be proper as well as impressive. A watch that did not have to be wound every day would be a gift that she would treasure. But as the jeweler showed him several models he felt that the price was a bit out of his range. He asked the salesperson to bring out the least expensive ladies' quartz watch that he had. Still the price was prohibitive. So he sighed, shrugged his shoulders and realized that since quartz was out of the question..........and then I pointed my finger toward the speakers. Mark listened to the tune, quickly understood the humor, and quietly said his usual, "okay, okay," and, as ever, trying to hide a smile. It might as well be spring.

Several patients who had been in the practice for so many years enjoyed an ongoing stream of joviality which would flow from visit to visit. We would engage in repartee that was often borderline flippant but never disparaging and certainly not offensive. One participant was a friend, named Zackary Garr, a man who had spent his working years in the road maintenance department of the state of Connecticut. He had a slow, measured way of engaging in verbal skirmishes which belied his quick mind. Soft spoken, it was as though he could taste every word as he formed his thinly-veiled insults. Once, at the beginning of his appointment, he placed some water on my operating stool, which was unbeknownst to me until I sat down. I pretended to be oblivious as he waited for my response. I had to retaliate, so I said I had a question to ask before I began working. "What was your family name before your father shortened it so that you would be able to spell it?" Another time, when he needed his next appointment sooner than my schedule allowed, he told my secretary that he could be called anytime at work should a cancellation arise, since the state garage was only ten minutes away. I told him that we could not do that, for we do not like to disturb anybody while they are sleeping.

But on one occasion he played the ultimate prank. He was a fan of the New York teams: Yankees, Jets, Giants, Rangers and Knicks. My devotion was to the Boston Red Sox, Celtics, Bruins and New England Patriots. So through the years we would often bet on games involving our favorites, and the wager was either a six-pack of beer or a bottle of vodka. After the Red Sox had beaten the Yankees for the American League pennant in that miracle year of 2004, he owed me a 1.75 liter pf Absolut. That was a big series, so we bet a big bottle. Two days later, while walking to the front desk with a patient, I saw Zack seated in the waiting room. He was holding a large brown paper bag which I knew contained my winnings. Walking toward me, he handed me the package and left without making any comment. Later that evening I felt that a vodka and tonic would be a nice way to relax, so I opened my new prize and poured myself a drink to celebrate my victory. As I began to sip I realized that the mixture was bland and unsavory. I poured some more vodka over the ice cubes, but it was still tasteless. Then I drank a bit directly from the bottle. Surprise! It was plain water. He had opened the bottle cap, replaced the contents with water, and resealed it so neatly that it had appeared unopened. The next morning I called him at work and reminded him that altering alcohol-containing vessels was a federal offense, and he had until six o'clock to make restitution, a word that he could look up in any dictionary, before I took further action.

On several occasions the patients provided a moment of lightheartedness that served to cheer me up. One morning, close to lunch time, I heard footsteps in the hallway heading toward my room. It was one of my elderly patients, a woman named Blanche, whose family owned a large local farm. Marching past the reception desk and into my operatory, she placed a huge paper bag on the floor near the door. It was full of fresh corn. She smiled as she said, "Since you are now divorced I'm sure there's no one cooking nice meals for you. These were just picked. Go home, throw them into boiling water, and enjoy." Before I could thank her she turned around and left. Only in a small town!

Since Colchester was approximately half-way between Boston and New York, the existence of eleven top tier professional teams in the four major sports at both the east and west ends of Connecticut provided many a spark for lively discussion. Our debates were always interesting, and never mean-spirited. With those of mutual interest I would share in analysis of plays or players, delight in recalling spectacular plays or situations, and join in moments of commiseration when the fates were not smiling upon our beloved bunch. My passion for the Red Sox, Patriots and Celtics was shared by many. My disdain for the Yankees, Mets, Giants, Jets and Knicks was interwoven in my Roxbury-nurtured DNA and was joined by co-believers whose interest and discourse ranged from casual attention all the way to hardened zealots. With the Red Sox world series heartbreaks occurring every decade, my most common contestation was with my Yankee fan friends, but always in a setting of playful confrontation. I would tell them that I felt like a member of the Olympic javelin-catching team.

Fortunately, only once was the lightheartedness of the verbal skirmishes violated. It was the only time that it was not fun.

When the Red Sox finally broke "the curse" and won the World Series in 2004, so many of my friendly Yankee boosters congratulated me, some on the telephon, and a few even sent cards expressing happiness for me that my team had finally reached baseball's Mount Olympus. All except one. This gentleman was a hard-core Yankee fan who had always been disagreeable whenever the any Red Sox had any success. His dialogue often smacked of criticism, especially during the decade of the 90's when the New Yorkers won four World Series titles while the Red Sox continued to struggle. Quite often I would suggest that we do not discuss baseball during his visits, for it was becoming less light-hearted and even a bit fractious. But he was relentless, and when my assistant Barbara politely suggested that he stop, her request went unheeded. So as fate would have it, he had an appointment scheduled a few weeks after my beloved Boston gang swept the St. Louis Cardinals in four games to win their first title in 86 years. Sitting in the chair with a wry smile on his face, he said nothing as Barbara placed the dental napkin around his neck. Then, with a smirk on his lips, he held up two small plastic bags, each one containing some pennies. There was a bit of silence. As I tried to interpret the meaning of his action, he made the task easier. One bag held six and the other one held twenty-six. They represented the number of World Series victories for each team. When he realized that I understood the significance of the graphic contrast, he held the bags higher and shook them, smiling as the heavier one made more noise. Enough was enough! With almost one motion, I removed the dental bib, lifted up the arm of the chair, and pointed to the door. His arrogance suddenly turned into muted disbelief. As he arose I suggested that he take his thirty two cents and buy a few lollipops, so that he can develop a few cavities for his new dentist to fill. I never saw him again. My cousin Sidney's philosophy of practice, which he had expressed many years before, came to mind. "Dentistry would be great if it were not for people."

There were quite a few baseball fan patients who were devotes of other teams, and I always looked forward to the friendly banter which our differences often promoted. The sport provides a wonderful framework for playful contention. The regular season is long, 162 games,, plus the playoffs and the eventual World Series match-up. One favorite nemesis was a dedicated Yankee fan named Cheryl, a patient of more than 30 years, who always scheduled her dental hygiene appointments in April and October, dates which coincided with major league Spring training and World Series time. And for more than a decade, October was a month where the Yankees excelled. At the beginning of each season we would offer our forecasts regarding individual as well as team performances: which player would have a higher batting average, who would hit more home runs, who would have a better pitching record, as well as where the Yankees and Red Sox would finish in the final standings. With a bit of bravado I would include the National League team that I believed the Red Sox would beat in the World Series. My hygienist (also named Sheryl) served as the official scribe, and attached a record of the predictions to Cheryl's dental record. Six months later, at the next hygiene visit we would check our results, and the winner would have bragging rights for about ten minutes. The decade of the 90's belonged to her, but from 2004 on I could put a smug smile on my face when I walked into the room for her dental exam. It was always great fun.

The gods of baseball must have been aligning the planets in 2003 in order to produce a most unusual synchronicity. My son Seth practices law in New Jersey, about an hour from Philadelphia. One weekend the Phillies were hosting the Boston Red Sox, so my son got tickets for us so that we could enjoy a day together rooting for our beloved hometown nine. We would also be sharing the experience of cheering on a visiting team in a hostile baseball city. As a bonus this was also a special event, for the Phillies were handing out a bobble-head doll of one of their Baseball Hall of Fame members, pitcher Steve Carlton. It was a most pleasurable afternoon, despite the fact that the Phillies were clobbering the

Red Sox. In addition to the lop-sided score, the Sox made a few embarrassing errors. But it was a day at the ballpark for a father and son, and that made it worthwhile.

But destiny was at work. A month later, Cheryl had an appointment with Sheryl. And once more, the baseball season was about to end without a pennant for my home town boys. As I walked into the hygiene room I greeted my Yankee fan buddy with a lament. I told her that not only was the season disappointing, but that I had been present at a Red Sox game in Philadelphia that was not only embarrassing but also very uncomfortable to watch. I was flabbergasted when Cheryl asked, "Was that by any chance the day they handed out Steve Carlton bobble-heads?" "How do you know about that ?" I asked. Her response shocked me. She was at the game! She was visiting friends in Philadelphia, and being a true baseball fan, took the opportunity to go to the game that day. The co-incidence jolted me, but it was her next remark, a real zinger, that I have since used as a standard with which to measure a person's true allegiance to any team in any sport at any age. She glanced at me with a look of respectful swagger, and in a menacing tone said, "If I knew you were there I would have hunted you down." Veterans Stadium had a seating capacity of 61,831. I do not know what the attendance was that day, but because of the doll give-away it was quite full. I told Cheryl that I was fortunate that she did not know that I was there. There is no doubt that she would have found me!

As I put pen to paper (or actually, tap keys on computer) to preface my next remarks, I was jolted by the phrase that just crossed my mind: in my half-century of practice. I use time measurement to describe my good fortune in building a support staff that remained with the office for many decades: Sue, one of my first hygienists who stayed for 40 years, Sheryl, another hygienist who was with us for 30 years, Valerie, a dental assistant who worked for 42 years, Penney, a secretary for over 25 years, another dental assistant named Sue who was with us for 25 years, and of course my Barbara who tolerated me for 18 years. There were a few who were unable to blend in with the office regimen or philosophy, and they left by mutual agreement. One was fired for dipping into the till, in the pre-computer days. One was discharged for constant absence and tardiness, and another for causing friction among co-workers. There were only two instances when my ire was aroused to the point that I resorted to sarcasm to teach a lesson.

The first occurred at the time Mike joined the practice. His schedule was designed to include working Wednesdays and Thursdays until 9 p.m. This extended the availability (the second of the three "A"s) of the office, so that now we could now announce to the community that the Colchester Dental Group was open six days plus two evenings per week. In interviewing applicants who had expressed an interest in joining the office to work alongside Mike, we realized that although the hours were a bit different, we would be able to identify a person who was qualified and could fit the schedule into her personal lifestyle. One of the candidates was a woman who had been working in another office in another town, but wanted to get a job closer to home. I explained to her that her hours would coincide directly with Mike's. If he were to finish early she could go home early, but if he had a problem and had to continue working a bit beyond the scheduled time, that she would have to remain at his side. Her response caught me off-guard. "I understand. But I must be home in time to watch Knots Landing." Her display of non-professionalism and her attitude of haughtiness pushed the sarcasm button in my head. "Miss, I guarantee you will be home in time to watch Knots Landing. You also will be home in time to watch Sesame Street, Howdy Doody, and Pee-Wee's Playhouse." I smiled as she walked out.

For many years we employed a local high school junior or senior to work after school hours as a file clerk...our "high school kid". This benefitted everybody, since the position gave the youngsters an opportunity to earn some money while getting some idea of how a business works. And then they would go on to other ventures, such as college and/ or full-time employment. Two of our youngsters became so interested in the work that was going on around them that they chose to become dental hygienists. We were so proud. But one time we had hired a senior who, in the beginning, performed her duties well, but became a bit testy as her tenure approached its end. She had been accepted to a fine university, and suddenly began to display a pompous attitude that became annoying to the staff. As her level of co-operation dropped we quickly organized a farewell party in our staff lounge. There was a cake with the perfunctory "good luck" written in frosting, and the obligatory greeting card signed by all. Again, the sarcasm button tripped, and instead of just signing my name, I inscribed a poem, which I borrowed from the comedian Nipsey Russell. It caused her great embarrassment, but the staff enjoyed the moment. It reads:

"Pursue some knowledge, go on to college, and stay there 'til you are through.

If they can make penicillin out of moldy bread, they can make something out of you."

On one occasion I was tempted to address a problem with a bit of sternness, but felt that it could be handled with a small dose of muffled sarcasm. One of Mike's early assistants was a competent employee, efficient, but usually unsmiling and often with a bit of a complaint. One day I walked into the lab and was immediately confronted with her gripe du jour: why does not everyone clean up after themselves when they are through polishing dentures? There was indeed a small mess on the counter, but, after all, it was a busy office. I looked at her and said, "I want you to know you are in my prayers every night." She peered at me with disbelief, until I finished my thought: "I thank God I'm not married to you." After a brief pause, she actually smiled...message received. We remained quasi-friends for a few more years.

There were three occasions when I took a brief hiatus from the practice and volunteered my services for a week or so in distressed areas. One venture was to Belize, a few miles from its boundary with Guatemala, where a clinic had been set up to provide medical and dental care for refugees who had crossed over the border.

But my trips to Haiti were the most fulfilling and soul-satisfying of all my travels, providing rewards that cannot be measured. The Haitian Health Foundation, in conjunction with the Diocese of Norwich had set up a presence in that distressed nation in the 1980's. The HHF was in the process of building a clinic in the town of Jeremie, on the western tip of the island. But before the structure had been completed, teams of volunteers, mostly from eastern Connecticut, traveled to remote villages, performing extractions outdoors, with only sunlight as the dental lamp and wicker chairs for the seating of patients.

On the first day I was taken in a pick-up truck to work in a nearby hamlet I was accompanied by Norman Cooper, a pharmacist from Norwich who had volunteered to be my dental assistant. Bishop Daniel Reilly also came with us, both to observe, to act as translator and to minister to the cluster of natives, who had crowded around our makeshift office, both to indulge their curiosity and to hope for treatment before the sun went down. When twilight approached and our day was finished I handed out trinkets to the group of youngsters who encircled me, hugging, touching my arms, smiling and shouting, "Papa, papa," which was their way of demonstrating respect and admiration. Although I understood the significance of the moment, I turned to Bishop Reilly and jokingly asked, "Why are they calling me papa? I've never been here before." He laughed. That was about as risque as I dared be with a man of the cloth.

A year later I returned to Haiti with my son Seth, who accompanied me for the week and functioned as my dental assistant. He was in law school at the time, and, being the kind, compassionate young man that he was (and still is), was so moved by my account of the first venture that he had developed a strong desire to participate. At different times several other dentists had brought their offspring along to share the experience with them. It exemplifies the meaning of the word bonding. I can recall one very hot day when our work was finished, and as we were cleaning up and disinfecting our instruments, a young native lad shinnied up a tree to shake a few cocoanuts to the ground. He brought two over, and cut them in half with a machete. I can still taste the sweet cocoanut milk and the crunch of the moist copra. A cocktail hour in a jungle setting, overlooking the Caribbean. It was a scene that will never appear in travel magazines.

Another memorable moment was brought about because of Seth's enjoyment of photography. One morning he arose at sunrise, to go about the area taking pictures in the early morning light. As our group sat at breakfast a bit later, Sister Carla, the administrator, noticed Seth's absence and asked me where he was. Before I could answer, Bishop Reilly, with his eyes twinkling and a smile growing wider as he spoke, stood up and in his booming Irish brogue announced that Seth was seen at the foot of the hill, hanging up a sign that read: "I am a lawyer, and will be here for one week. If you have been injured by your dentist, please contact me." Bishop Riley's wit was as easily demonstrated as was his sense of compassion and kindness. Both he and Seth provided me with an abundance of cherished memories.

A few years before I retired I volunteered (actually, was volunteered) to deliver a presentation on dental care to a combined group of kindergartners and first graders in Needham, Massachusetts. My grandchildren Simon and Zoe had planned this with their teachers, and my daughter Elyse was kind enough not only to accept for me, but also to inform me about a week before the scheduled presentation. There was no way that I could possibly evade the honor. So I created a lecture kit that consisted of a large toothbrush and a model of the upper and lower teeth that my hygienists used for patient education. Then I filled a package with small tubes of toothpaste, a few dozen small containers of dental floss, and a few handfuls of toothbrushes. I did not bring patient education brochures, for they were not yet able to read.

But what would I say to my mini-audience? Public speaking had become rather easy for me through the years. As chairperson of the Colchester Board of Education, I had delivered graduation speeches for each of nine years, and had presented educational budgets to the town during each of my sixteen years on the school board. As chairperson of the Colchester Democratic Town

Committee for nearly a decade, I would need only about 30 seconds to prepare an address to a gathering of any size. On three separate occasions I delivered nominating speeches at the Connecticut Democratic State conventions, and even, as chairperson of the Credentials Committee, certified the delegates and delivered the call for the proceedings to begin. Also, I once appeared on a panel discussion regarding educational funding on Connecticut Public Television. And there were about half a dozen testimonials and/or roasts where I was privileged to act as master of ceremonies. But I never stood before a group of mini-people to deliver a homily on dental hygiene. As Elyse was driving us to the school, she began to laugh hysterically. "I have heard you speak many times, and often quote a line that you had delivered at my own graduation, but I have never seen you so flustered before." I had to laugh. It was true.

On entering the classroom, I was greeted not only by the teachers, but was immediately surrounded by the little ones who were happy to inform me that they knew that I was Simon and Zoe's grandfather. I became an instant mini-celebrity. And then one lad asked me why my grandchildren called me Saba rather than Grandpa. Now I had to explain that when my first grandchild, Solomon, had been born many years earlier, I did not want to use an appellation that conjured up any sense of aging such as grandpa or gramps, so I chose to be called by the Hebrew word for grandfather which was Saba. But, of course, I explained it in much simpler terms. Then it was announced by one little girl that she had two cavities, and another said that she sometimes goes to bed without brushing her teeth because her mommy and daddy just want her to get to sleep right away. I listened without responding.

When they were finally herded into a circle and seated on the floor, the presentation began. After the usual demonstration of proper brushing of both upper and lower teeth and as well as cleansing the tongue, I cited examples of both good and bad foods and drinks. Also, I presented an uncomplicated description of the sequence of eruption and exfoliation of both deciduous and permanent dentition, of course using much simpler words. Seeing the audience becoming restless and anxious to talk, I opened the floor to discussion. I thought that would be a safe way to bring the event to a merciful close. One youngster asked me if asparagus was a healthy food, because I had not mentioned it. This led to another question regarding the merits of artichoke. Another asked about beer, because her father has one or two every night. One lad stood up and proclaimed that I was correct in my illustration of the proper use of floss, for he flosses twice a day and my example was perfect. Then I was told by one little tyke that my suggestion to place a small amount of toothpaste on the brush, a pea-sized measure, was not good, because he hated to eat peas. At that fortuitous moment I thanked the class for inviting me, offered my gratitude to the teachers for arranging the event, and told my daughter that she owed me a drink on the way home. As I look back, I realize that this, my last presentation to any group, was perhaps my finest. The smiles on my grandchildren's faces raised my serotonin level higher than any applause that I may have received for any speech on any topic at any time in any other place.

Another dental-related out of office episode occurred at a function sponsored by the Connecticut Sports Foundation, a celebrity dinner and auction that raises money for cancer patients and their families. It is an annual event, held at the Mohegan Sun Casino's Convention Center in Uncasville CT. The feature of the evening is a discussion conducted by several past and present major league baseball players, including a few members of baseball's Hall of Fame, who, during the cocktail hour, mingle with the guests, signing autographs and making small talk. After the meal they entertain questions from the audience about the sport. For years the New York Yankees have had the greater number of participants, and the master of ceremonies on that particular evening was a very prominent New York City sportscaster.

It was February, 2005, just a few months after my beloved Boston Red Sox made baseball history by defeating the Yankees to win the American League pennant, coming from three games behind to win the next four and then go on to win the World Series, their first in 86 years. It was a sweet victory for Red Sox fans, and for months they delighted in recalling the tale of how our heros brought fear, disbelief, and an embarrassing defeat to our passionately disliked rivals. At the meal, we were seated at a table with four other couples, two of whom were sporting Yankee shirts. My late wife, in an impish moment, announced to our table mates that I was a life-long Red Sox fan. Directly across from me a rather large gent, wearing a Yankee shirt and baseball cap, jumped up and in a voice lubricated by a few drinks demanded to know why there was a Red Sox fan at his table. I just looked at him and said that I was a dentist, trained in C.P.R., and was present in case anyone should begin to choke. Nobody laughed. The rest of the meal was very quiet.

As the staff grew through the years I was fortunate to be able to relate to them in a fashion that was an amalgamation of friendship and professionalism, jocularity and seriousness, and frivolity and respect. Having started my practice as a solo practitioner, without enough patients to treat or any money available to hire support personnel, it was a long journey from my first day when I would unlock the office door, put on the coffee, answer the phone, arrange the instruments, greet and seat the patient, mix my own materials, dismiss the patient, schedule the next appointment, collect the fee, clean and sterilize the instruments, prepare the operatory for the next patient, answer the phone, etc. By my last decade of practice the staff had grown to be comprised of two partners, three hygienists, five dental assistants, and three secretaries. Very fortuitous, for as my friend Dr. Babinski often reminded me, I did not know how make a good cup of coffee.

Although it is most important to treat all members of the dental team equally, there were always a few who, through their gullibility or naivete or just penchant for laughter, became easy targets for the occasional amusing banter that lightened the moment in a very busy and sometimes rigid environment.

Our bi-weekly staff meetings often provided a setting for lightheartedness, again designed to bring about a semblance of serenity in the middle of a busy day in the middle of a busy week. Although we used the sessions to update the staff on matters ranging from practice management problems, introductions to newer techniques, thoughts on improving the office, or even to determine the date and place of our annual Christmas party, there were also discussions of trivial matters, ranging from places in the parking lot all the way to types of snacks for the staff lounge or the choice of magazines to display in the reception area.

There was one over-riding rule: if anyone insulted another staff member, he or she would be fined one dollar, which went into a large coffee can (there's that coffee again) and would be donated to charity when the amount became respectable. For a while I was the largest contributor, often reacting to a statement or proposal with a smart-alecky remark that I could not hold back. To cite a few examples:

I'd like to help you out. Which way did you come in?

You are a fine example as to why some species eat their young.

You're funny....but looks aren't everything.

You are so confused that you probably think Einstein means one glass of beer.

Did your mother have any children that lived?

I tried to avoid a fine by recalling the immortal words of Charlie Chaplin, who summed up the value of his art form in a single sentence:"A day without laughter is a day wasted."

One of our secretaries was Penny, a delightful woman who spoke with a crisp British accent, and who had been with us for more that 25 years. Her self-assigned task was to bake a cake for the staff to enjoy when someone's birthday was near. One time we were celebrating multiple events, so she had "Happy Birthday All" inscribed in frosting. Early in the morning of the event she placed the cake on the kitchen table and covered it with a daintily-decorated napkin. Later, as the crew left to congregate in the reception area for the staff meeting, I altered the greeting a bit and re-covered the cake. Then, as we gathered around for a bit of refreshment, one of our newer staff members removed the cover, stared at the cake, and asked, "Who is Al?" Again, I was charged one dollar.

Only once was the fine doubled. Mike Babinski has a wonderful, eclectic sense of humor, and he and I spent many moments together enjoying a few recorded performances by the comedian Jackie Mason. Mike has a fine ear for dialect, and can duplicate Mason's accent and speech pattern so closely that a listener would think that Mike himself had just gotten off the proverbial boat and settled down on New York's lower east side. My partner also built a fairly substantial inventory of Mason-like utterances, complete with proper vocal inflections and hand gestures. So at one staff meeting I announced that as a gesture of appreciation for Mike's interest in learning Yiddish phrases, I would try to learn one expression each week pertaining to his own ethnic extraction (pun unintended). So this week's statement is "Two and two are ten." That cost me two dollars, despite my pleading that I was also laughing at myself, for my own grandmother had come to this country from Poland. My plea for literary levity license was ignored. I paid the fine. With no more dollars in my pocket, I had to remain quiet for the rest of the meeting.

Staff longevity was a two-fold blessing. For the patients, seeing the same familiar faces for years brought a degree of comfort, both because it represented stability and also fostered a sense of friendliness and trust. For me, it became the tapestry upon which relationships between co-workers could be woven, and provided a few different levels of interaction. They were always available as a quasi-audience for puns that came to mind on the spur of the moment and might be used later in the day. My attempt was always to try to create a light-hearted atmosphere in an environment that could easily become a bit tense or rushed, with two partners, three hygienists, five dental assistants, three secretaries always engaged in some type of activity with a group of people called patients. Joviality always had value. And involving patients directly in a moment of amusement was akin to opening a window in a smoky room.

In my early years of practice, especially the first decade as a solo practitioner, the relationship between myself and my employees was formal. This was the typical atmosphere in any professional office, be it dental, medical, legal, etc. Proper attire was dictated not only by the seriousness of the setting (both real and perceived), but also by the perception of proper decorum befitting the dignified nature of the environment as so often portrayed both in movies and in popular literature. Conjure up the names of Dr. Kildare or Perry Mason and an image will come to mind. One byproduct of the tumultuous 60's was the relaxation of structure in both relationships and assumed decorum. My starched white uniform outfits were replaced by colorful scrubs. Dental assistants' attire expanded to include slacks and polychromatic outfits. And my growing staff and I were able to morph a conventional setting into one that was characterized more by congeniality than prescribed conventionality. First names were used and relaxation of long-standing mores occurred. Although high standards of patient care, coupled with involvement in continuing education were never compromised, laughter was now heard with a greater frequency. It produced something of an enigma...I looked forward to Monday mornings....I was going to work. To underscore my good fortune, research has shown that the greatest number of heart attacks among men occurred on Monday mornings. But I went to the office feeling quite happy!

Sue was one of my first dental hygienists, and was still with my office on my final day forty years later. Her gentle nature, coupled with a kind persona and an innocent trust that sometimes led to gullibility provided an on-going setting for light-heartedness, which her patients truly enjoyed. I was able to josh with her without generating an iota of denigration, and often the laughter coming from the room could be heard by my secretaries at the front desk. To allay any possibility of anxiety that often occurs when the doctor walks into a room to examine a patient and review current clinical findings, Sue and I would often engage in a moment or two of amusing dialogue. Praising Sue, I would say that, "She could light up a room....by leaving it." Or that, "if the whole world were made up of Sue Halls it would be a better place. You would know everybody's name." "I've known Sue for forty years, and I still can't stand her." Sue would always laugh, for both she and the patient knew that her skill as a hygienist was unquestioned. My respect for her was always evident.

Since her room was immediately adjacent to mine there were many moments during the day when I could toss off a remark while passing by that would immediately produce a hearty laugh. Once, while making her lunch, Sue left a frozen dinner too long in the kitchen microwave, causing severe overheating and resulting in a billow of smoke pouring out when she opened the oven door. It also created a moment of embarrassment in front of the staff. So, never wanting to miss an opportunity, a day later I walked past her room to say good morning. She looked, and then began to laugh hysterically. I was carrying a fire extinguisher over my shoulder. To add to her fluster Sue had to explain to the patient who was seated in the dental chair and facing away from the door what was so funny at that moment.

Over four decades there were many instances when playfulness was apropos. In my early years, and with a small staff, I would write out the weekly pay checks, since I did not yet need a payroll service and tax computation was a simple matter. One day Sue came to me and with a saddened face showed me a shriveled wad of paper. She had left her check in the pocket of her uniform and without realizing it had put it into her washing machine. That crumpled mass was all that was left. So I generated a replacement. Sure enough, a few weeks later she did it again, and sheepishly handed me another scrap that once was her salary. So once again I wrote out a duplicate, but before I handed it to her I went over to my closet, removed the washing instruction label from a shirt, and taped it to her check. No conversation was necessary.

Self-denigration, making myself the target, was a technique I often used to create a moment of relaxation. But one time Sue came up with a line that was funny both for its timing and its pseudo-attempt to be an insult. To help create a relaxed atmosphere, I would often tell a patient that one of my most precious attributes and one that helped me keep on an even keel was that, "I gave myself the ability to laugh at myself." One day I uttered that favorite line and received a bit of a jolt. Sue's response was immediate, and evened the score: "He gave that ability to everybody."

April Fool's Day was one that required caution in my office. The staff was very alert to the possibility that something was going to happen to somebody sometime during the day. Sue Hall was a perennial target. One unusual prank was actually conjured up by my assistant Barbara. We filled six vinyl gloves with ice cubes, and tucked them under the rear tires of Sue's car. At the end of the day we gathered at a window and watched as she got into her vehicle. Sue shifted into reverse, and slowly backed out. As the car began to move the rear end suddenly lifted into the air. She set the brake and ran out, not knowing what had happened, until we emerged laughing from the office.

Another time I had squirted a bit of toothpaste into the earpiece of her wall phone, and a few moments later called her on the intercom. She told us the next day that when she got home her young daughter asked her, "What's the green stuff in your ear Mommy?" An easy caper consisted of parking my car so close to the driver's side of Sue's so that she could not get in to drive home until she came back into the office and asked nicely for assistance. This was used only if she had been a bit flippant during the day. But one time she felt emboldened, and enlisted the aid of her last patient, who had already been treated and examined, but still sat in the chair with the napkin around her neck. Sue signaled me to come into her operatory, while she went out to the sink in the hall to clean her instruments. As I passed by I felt a stream of water hit my legs, and watched the choreographed exit as the patient dismissed herself and Sue quickly ran out the door. One minute later I received a call from Sue. She was at the end of the driveway, but had wanted to say goodbye. I'd been had!

On another April 1 date I received a signal on the message board behind me that someone was trying to contact me. As I removed my mask and gloves and turned away from the patient to pick up the phone, I was startled to hear what was coming from the earpiece. It was slow, rhythmic, repeated heavy breathing. I had received an obscene intercom call! It was easy to trace the communication. It was my secretary Penny. Her voice was easily distinguishable, and although the only communication was the sound of someone's breath, her impish smile that reflected a playful nature gave her away. I walked up to her desk and just stared. She broke into laughter. She would have been a prime suspect anyway, for she was one of the best participants in the spontaneous water-pistol shooting sprees that erupted every now and then, at the end of a day when we needed a tension release.

But Penny was the perpetrator of the best April Fool's Day prank that ever sand-bagged me. It was a chilly, cloudy morning, and had been raining heavily for a few hours. I parked my car in my usual spot, near the rear door to my private office. The staff had their own entrance, which opened into the employee lounge. My door was always unlocked. The ladies usually arrived earlier, and someone would unfasten it so that I could enter quickly, especially if the weather was foul or if I had an armful of office supplies that I had purchased the night before. As I ran through a downpour I reached for the door handle and turned it quickly, hoping to minimize getting soaked. The door would not open. The handle just kept turning and turning, but nothing would happen. So instinctively, I took out my office keys and tried to unlock the door, but nothing was helping. I grabbed the door knob again, and noticed that I was not gripping the knob. It kept slipping in my hand. Penny had covered the mechanism with a large amount of vaseline, which in my haste I had not noticed and was also not evident because of the heavy rain pounding against the door. A few moments later the door opened. Penny and the other early arrivals had been watching the entire event through a window in the staff lounge. Someone was dispatched to rescue me. It was so clever and so well orchestrated that I had to laugh. After all, it was I who long ago had set the tone for shenanigans.

Will Rogers once said that "everything is funny, as long as it's happening to someone else." That was proven the time a well-devised April Fools prank made me the playee rather than the player. Barbara had conspired with one of my secretaries to create a practical joke that would be certain to give me a jolt. Using a digital camera, they took pictures of each other. They then magnified the two photos on a computer until they became life-size replicas. Just before I left to go home the two conspirators taped them onto the rear window of my car, with the faces placed toward the inside. As I left work, and without noticing them, I got into my vehicle, buckled my seat belt and turned on the engine. When I looked into the rear view mirror before backing up I literally jumped in my seat. I saw two very stern faces staring at me. It took a few very long seconds before I realized that I was now the victim. I had to go back into the office and congratulate them. They reminded me of a popular adage that warns, "If you want to play you have to pay."

And then there was the one that backfired. Barbara always parked her Land Rover with its rear end against the wall of the building, to provide an easy egress. A perfect setting for one of the oldest of all practical jokes, the act of tying tin cans to the rear bumper of a car so that they might create a noise that would puzzle the driver, perhaps signaling a problem that would then cause the person to stop immediately. So I fastened ten empty containers of varying sizes, and later watched through a window as Barbara began to drive off. I expected her to brake immediately. But she continued on cautiously around the building and began to cross the large parking lot, heading slowly toward the driveway and then onto the street. I ran outside and quickly realized why I had failed. The engine of her vehicle was so loud that she was unaware of any clatter coming from behind. I ran toward her, waving my arms as a signal to stop, which she did just as she was about to turn into the main flow of traffic. She quickly stepped out and asked what had caused me to run after her. Sheepishly I began to remove the noisemakers, and quietly walked back to my own car. Suddenly I recalled a line from Robert Burns that I had enjoyed reciting in its original form so many years back in a course in English literature: "The best laid schemes of mice and men gang aft agley." Had I majored in engineering rather than English I would have certainly known that a Land Rover diesel engine with a Garrett T2 turbocharger makes quite a racket!

My personal hygienist, Sheryl Postemski, was a quieter, methodical, placid person. Always soft spoken, she went about her business in a most exemplary way. Her kindness and gentle approach endeared her to the patients. Having grown up on a farm, she was knowledgeable about so many aspects of life in a rural area that she developed a kinship with people that lasted for decades. At first, it took me a while to become used to her tranquil way of speaking, to the extent that I often had to ask her to repeat a sentence. This was a common occurrence. My solution was to purchase a large plastic megaphone, which I placed in a corner of her room. When she was in the midst of reporting her evaluation of the patient's oral health and her voice began to modulate lower, I had only to point my finger toward the cone-shaped object standing against the wall. Message received. She made the dialogue audible again. Silent communication was used to increase spoken volume.

Once, when I had a sore throat which was the last remnant of a bad cold, my voice was a bit quieter than usual, setting the scene for a bit of unexpected humor. It took place when, after I had examined one of Sheryl's patients, the two of us began to discuss a treatment plan. We were facing each other, and we were both speaking in low tones. After a minute or two passed the patient sat up in the chair, stared at us, and exclaimed, "Can you two actually hear each other?" With the sound of background music mixed with the usual noise of a busy office that comes wafting into the room, the patient could see our lips moving, but could not hear any meaningful bits of conversation.

Quite often, when I was her hygiene patient, I would fall asleep in her chair. The combination of a relaxing hour in the office coupled with her gentle way of speaking provided a mellow atmosphere, and so I would close my eyes and almost immediately drift off. Sheryl often described my routine when talking to anxious patients, as an example of how it could actually be pleasant to have one's teeth cleaned. She would reinforce her theory by recalling the moment when she gently tapped me on my shoulder to wake me from my light sleep. She was finished, and asked me to rinse. "Do I have to?" was my response. That was also a tribute to her gentle touch.

Since I have a passion for gardening I found her to be an excellent source of information. We would spend some time at the beginning of each planting season to exchange ideas about our favorite time of the year. A few months into my retirement I received an e-mail from her. The date was March 16th. Sheryl had sent me a brief reminder that, "Tomorrow is St. Patrick's Day. Don't forget to plant your peas." We had joked about that tradition for decades, but to honor her friendship I followed her instructions. It was the first time that I had ever started the growing season so early, but it turned out to be quite effective. Best crop of peas ever. She was more excited than I was. She was such a dear friend.

Doreen was a delightful secretary who was with our practice for only a year, due to her husband's unexpected change of job location that took them across the country. But in that short period she charmed us with her soft, soothing southern accent. Always polite and proper, she did surprise me once with her understated display of wit. At the end of one particularly hectic day, as I was saying goodbye to her, I remarked that the schedule had been so packed that I was a bit drained. "No rest for the wicked," she said. When I corrected her by saying that I believed the expression was actually, "No rest for the weary," she looked directly at me and with a bit of a smile commented, "I call 'em as I see 'em." I enjoyed her gentle poke. We all loved her.

And then there was Joyce, an excellent patient co-ordinator who was with us for more than a decade, but also had to leave when her husband's job had him transferred to another state. Joyce was an extremely personable woman who had an unusual ability to relate to everyone in a way that immediately smacked of kindness as well as helpfulness. Efficient beyond expectation, and with a wonderful sense of humor, her uprightness, coupled with a trusting, almost gullible nature, made her an easy target for buffoonery. She had an eclectic sense of humor, and as a devout Catholic she chuckled when I told her that a favorite pick-up line in my high school days was to ask a girl on a Friday if she needed something to talk about at confession that Sunday. She would look at me and say, almost in disbelief, "Oh my G-d." But it was obvious that there was never any semblance of offensiveness or disrespect.

However, there was one time when she did not speak to me for a few days. I was escorting an elderly woman to the front desk to set up her next appointment. As we approached Joyce's station, my patient began to praise her, saying aloud how pleasant Joyce was, how she had helped with the appointments and was so kind and efficient in explaining and making financial arrangements. Joyce smiled as the accolades kept coming. A few more compliments; a few more smiles. Then I remarked that, "We could not get along without Joyce." Joyce smiled even more. And I continued, "But then again, we could not get along without toilet paper." Joyce stopped smiling. For the rest of the week any dialogue between us was strictly professional, relating only to the practice schedule and patient flow. Her words were measured, but her eyes were focused like two laser beams. "It's that darn funnel again."

In my last few years we were joined by a secretary named Becky, who eventually became our office manager. Slim, brown-eyed, she was a very bright woman who was super-efficient at her job, quite professional, and yet always had a bit of a devilish twinkle in her eyes. When an injection of tomfoolery was welcome to decrease a backdrop of tension, or even boredom, she would invite a change of attitude by looking at me with an impish smile and announce, "Game's on." That would result in a morning or afternoon spent looking for playful pitfalls throughout the office. Something might be booby-trapped, and I had to be very careful as I moved about throughout the day. She also had a few other targets, and my hygienist Sue was near the top of the list. One day Becky attached a large artificial, nasty-looking and grossly-textured slug to the handle of Sue's car. Then she invited us to watch with her through the window as Sue left for home, went to open her car door, and found herself holding a strange, fleshy varmint in her hand. Becky laughed as Sue moved quickly away from her car and let out a bit of a shriek. All she had to do was give me a whimsical glance, and I would be on guard for the rest of the week.

Confucius once stated, "Choose a job you love and you will never have to work a day in your life." That sentiment was echoed centuries later by a vaudeville performer named Nathan Birnbaum, who gained fame after he changed his name to George Burns. As he began to approach 100 years of age, he was often asked the secret of longevity. His response was both concise and instructive: "You can't help getting older, but you don't have to get old." Very powerful. I took that to heart, and whenever I was asked where I grew up, my answer always was, "I haven't yet."

He also believed that, "You should fall in love with your work." This was always my credo, and it was oft quoted during my professional career. But the melody of life is a tune created by the rhythm of a ticking clock, a sound that occasionally comes to the foreground as a signal for the baton to begin slowing down, not to end the symphony, but merely to change the tempo. When I was in my seventies people would sometimes ask me when I was going to retire. So many of them were looking forward to their own work-free days so that they could not understand why I was still on the job. My reply was simplistic, but also realistic: "Before my eyes begin to go, or my hands begin to shake, or my jokes fall flat." And I would add that perhaps I had them in the wrong order. My eyes were still quite good (I had lens implants inserted a decade before), and my hands were always so steady that occasionally my staff or my partners would remark about their quality.

Quite often, when I would be performing a delicate procedure which I was obviously admiring as it was unfolding, Barbara would say to the patient, "He's showing off again." And then she would add, "I love to watch. His hand is like a rock." A few times I would use my opposite hand to add a final touch. When Barbara first saw my demonstration of quasi-ambidexterity she was impressed and praised my prowess. "Was that a left-handed compliment?" I asked. Once in a while, and with the correct patient in the chair, I would disclose that I knew I had good hands way back in my high school years. "There were many times when I was on a date and my lady friend would tell me to watch my hands. I was not able to use that line with most individuals,

It was ironic that although I had chosen age 80 as a fine time to end one career and begin another, it was the third aspect of the triad noted above, jokes falling flat, that told me that my decision was timely (pun intended). Once in a while a few well known and oft-quoted lines from Shakespeare that I had read and dissected in college came wafting across my mind: "Life's but a walking shadow, a poor player that struts and frets his hour upon the stage, and then is heard no more...." As the play which we call life unfolds, there are distinct acts with diverse plots and sub-plots, all governed by a defined period of time. The trick is to take a bow before the curtain closes and sweeps one aside, or even away.

For years I had related a fabricated account of Alexander The Great, king of Macedon, an historical giant who had conquered one-third of the world in the third century BC. He needed a way to measure time so that he could co-ordinate the movements of his great armies across vast lands, so he charged his wizards to devise a method for performing this task. After many days of experimentation it was discovered by his experts that a strip of wool, when dipped into various dyes, would hold the color for a definite unit of time, and then quickly fade. Some lasted a few hours, and some held their color much longer, even a day or two. Many swatches could then be treated with several different pigments and when sewn together would create a multi-colored fabric. Thus, by observing and comparing the duration of the color fastness, they had in essence created a functional timepiece. To complete the project, this could be fashioned into a cuff that Alexander could wear on his wrist. And this was the history of Alexander's Ragtime Band.

For many, many years, this would always bring a chuckle from the patient. The premise was easily recognizable, for that song was a part of our musical culture, remembered by many and often incorporated in the movies as a tuneful background to the roaring 20's. But as the years progressed I noticed that the recognition factor had diminished to the point that I now reserved its recollection for senior citizens and music afficionados. But slowly, slowly, many other punfully-engineered bits of historical recollections had to be either explained or just passed off with a shrug. Everybody always reacted gleefully to my concocted account of Columbus' five ships. In addition to the three that everybody knew and even as school-children could name, because they crossed the ocean to the new world,most were unaware of the two that had sailed a day earlier. They are forgotten because they fell off the edge before it was discovered that the world was round. Fabrications of that nature always brought a response.

But the passage of time put a dull edge onto what once quite easily produced a sharp observation and a predictable response. For example, a whimsical reference to the powerful political presence of Lyndon Johnson that was so strong in the 1960s that it quite often cast a shadow over his vice-president, led to the witty alteration of a popular song title that was revised to read "On A Clear Day You Can See Hubert." That reference, in later years, often resulted in a blank stare. The history books have immortalized Christopher Columbus so that he is known to every sixth-grader, but Hubert Humphrey is familiar mainly to senior citizens and students of history.

"What's past is prologue," wrote Shakespeare in The Tempest. All of life up to now is actually an introduction to the beginning of a new journey. The past records the present and sets the stage for the future. A few weeks before my last day of practice I had a moment in time that was for me the paramount of example of an epiphany. It took a few seconds for me to understand its meaning, and thus reassure myself that all was right and to realize that in that instant I had received a divine message telling me that my life was on its proper course. It involved another contrived story. My paternal heritage has been traced back to Holland, where my son Seth and daughter-in-law Rachel have identified Parks way back to the mid 1600's. My forebears had earned their living as cigar-makers. This was a rich background for fabrication, so I invented a story of my great-great grandfather who owned a tulip farm. Everyday my great-great-grandmother would tend to the shop and take orders from customers as they passed by. Then my great-great grandfather would trudge up the hill to the flower beds, fill his basket with the desired number of flowers, and walk down the hill toward the shop to complete the sale. As he grew older the trip up and down the embankment became quite difficult. To make his task easier, he attached a cable to a tree at the edge of the tract and brought the other end down to the shop, where he secured it to a post. Now he could remain in the field. When a customer wanted to make a purchase, my great-great-grandmother would shout out the order to my great-great-grandfather. He would then place the items in his basket, secure it to the line with a pulley and send it down the incline to the store. And thus it was my ancestor who invented flowers by wire.

Synchronicity is the experience of two or more events which are causally unrelated occurring together in a meaningful way. This provided me with the one special moment when I realized that it really was time to hang up the drill. The last addition to our staff was a very young dental assistant named Julie who had recently completed her training, and had joined our practice just a few months before I announced my retirement date. She was a warm, congenial person who, in short time, became quite adept at her job. Polite, pleasant and professional, patients always felt at ease with her. With a constant smile on her face, and soon feeling quite secure in her employment, Julie would, on occasion, respond to one of my comedic conversational concoctions with a retort of her own. She had an impish sense of humor, and would come back at me immediately with a quip in response. Then her large dark eyes would open just a bit wider, and she would present a look that was a combination of joyful self-approval mixed with a quizzical moment when she appeared to question whether she might have been a bit too flippant or even disrespectful. I quickly assured her that I enjoyed the exchange, and always praised her for her quick wit. And to underscore my pleasure I often added, "That was very good....just don't get ahead of me kid."

One morning Julie came into my operatory with some sterilized instruments. As she was placing them in the drawer I began to tell her the tale of my great-great-grandfather in Holland. With an air of pride, and speaking in a slow, definitive tone, I declared that it was he who, "invented flowers by wire." I looked at her in disbelief, for she just glanced back and forth between Barbara and myself, obviously wondering what it was that I was trying to tell her. Suddenly Barbara began to laugh hysterically. "She has no idea what you are talking about. Her generation never heard of flowers by wire. They go to their computers and order on-line." Bingo! My hands are still steady, my eyes are still good, but a great joke fell flat! The signal for the end of another act.

. Okay. Time to begin another venture. I was an English major in college. Writing was always enjoyable, and through the years I would often sit and compose poems as a means of relaxation. In addition, seeing my name in print as well as getting paid to produce some free-lance articles was always enjoyable. And I can still work, while also enjoying the luxury of lingering in bed just a bit longer in the morning. As I reflect back on my dental experiences and years of practice I realize that there were so many funny moments. Laughter in a dental office? An oxymoron? People never link dentistry with humor. I can do that and at the same time accomplish a life-long dream. With so much more free time in every day, I think I will write a book.

EPILOGUE

I Already Played the Ed Sullivan Show

Time is a unit, a quantity that is measured by mechanical means and devices. Its true valuation can only be determined when the concept is linked to substantive events or occurrences. To illustrate my premise, I admit that as I matured (which many refer to as 'growing old') I found myself fascinated by the ever-increasing number of years marked off on the calendar, so much that I would try to grasp the feeling and true meaning of the passage of time by devising my personal theory of relativity. It is quite a bit simpler than the famous one devised by Professor Einstein. Subtracting 54, the length of my dental career, from 1935, the year of my birth, takes me back to 1881, a mere number until I mix in some meaningful events: President James Garfield was both inaugurated and assassinated. Clara Barton founded the Red Cross, Chief Sitting Bull surrendered to U. S. troops in Montana, Billy the Kid was shot by Pat Garrett, and the University of Connecticut was founded. That's a lot of years! I then knew what 54 years felt like.

And when I subtract the years of my life from the year of my birth, I am transported way back to 1854. That was also a memorable year in our history: Franklin Pierce was president, Henry David Thoreau published "Walden", the U. S. Naval Academy was established at Annapolis, Maryland, the Boston Public Library opened its doors, and the Republican Party was formed. As I commingle substantive entities such as well-known historical events with years that are defined only by numbers, I can produce a personal feeling for the passage of time.

In looking back at one's life it is predictable, and quite acceptable, for a person to add just a tinge of remorse to its recollection. Change is central to the universe. In writing this there were moments when I felt just a dash of melancholy, for there were so many wonderful reminiscences that will never be reenacted or recaptured. Time passes without leaving mile markers. In searching for inspirational guidelines on conducting one's life, an individual can find wisdom that stretches across the centuries. About 500 BC the Greek philosopher Heraclitus defined both the value and the significance of a moment by his simple observation that a person cannot swim in the same river twice. And an optimistic similarity was noted in the 1930's by Mae West, when she proclaimed that, "you only live once, but if you do it right, once is enough." Add to that the simple lyrics of my favorite song, sung by Frank Sinatra, "My Way," and you have an approach for measuring success in any venture.

I had to go fifty years back in time to realize that retrospection also has a positive aspect. On September 17th, 1967, the rock band The Doors was scheduled to appear on the super-popular Ed Sullivan television show. An appearance on that weekly program usually brought immediate fame to new performers. Since it was designated as a family program at a time when the country was undergoing a change of social mores, the producers kept a close rein on the content of every act. The group was scheduled to sing their new hit "Light My Fire". About fifteen minutes before air time they were told that one line would have to be changed: "girl we couldn't get much higher" was deemed inappropriate for their show because of its association with illegal drug use. The group discussed it, and under the pressure of the moment, consented to a change of wording. However, as they began to sing it was obvious to them that the artistic quality of their work was being compromised. It was their creation, and so they sang the original, although forbidden, version. Mr. Sullivan showed displeasure and a discernable look of anger on his face as they were taking their bows, despite the fact that he audience gave them a rousing ovation.

When the broadcast had ended, the producer burst into their dressing room, and in an angry tone of voice told them that because they had not conformed to the moral standards that were prescribed, they would never again be allowed to perform on the Ed Sullivan Show. Jim Morrison, the lead singer, looked at him, pushed aside any thoughts of a contentious response to the man's anger, and with a shrug of his shoulder just said, "Hey man, we just did the Ed Sullivan show."

Although it was expressed in a simple fashion, Morrison's reply had an impact on me. "Been there, done that," was a popular phrase that was coined decades later, and can refer to anything, ranging from going on an African safari or simply taking one's first bite of an anchovy pizza. But to have "played the Ed Sullivan Show" represents the pinnacle of life's efforts and experiences. Looking back should not bring about a feeling of regret that the time has passed, but rather a sense of gratitude and that it was well spent, well accepted, and produced a beneficial result. About 300 years ago Jonathan Swift took a break from writing satire and turned to philosophy, when he penned a line that is both a prayer and an instruction: "May you live all the days of your life." If you do, your book can close with a happy ending.

Printed in the United States
By Bookmasters